UNDERSTANDING
WOMEN

UNDERSTANDING WOMEN

A FEMINIST PSYCHOANALYTIC APPROACH

LUISE EICHENBAUM
SUSIE ORBACH

Basic Books, Inc., Publishers

NEW YORK

First published as **Outside In, Inside Out** by Penguin Books, Middlesex, England, in 1982. This expanded version published in 1983.

Library of Congress Cataloging in Publication Data

Eichenbaum, Luise.
   Understanding women.

   Expanded version of: Outside in, inside out.
1982.
   Bibliography: p. 200.
   Includes index.
   1. Feminist therapy.   2. Psychoanalysis—
Social aspects.   3. Women—Psychology.
I. Orbach, Susie, 1946-   . II. Title.
RC489.F45E38   1983   616.89'14'088042   82-72545
ISBN 0-465-08864-3

CONTENTS

Contents

PREFACE

ON the morning of April 6, 1976, we deposited a hundred envelopes in the mailbox outside Chalk Farm Tube Station, London. In each one was a letter and a leaflet announcing the opening of The Women's Therapy Centre in Islington on April 8. The mailing went to women's groups, women's centers, doctors in the area, educational institutions, psychiatric clinics, and national and local media. We were nervous and excited, eager to see the response. Later that day we took possession of the Centre's premises and, paint rollers in hand, kerchiefs on our heads, we spruced up two therapy rooms and an administrative office. Friends came to help and we chatted excitedly about our plans for the Centre. We were opening it, we said, because women wanted psychotherapeutic services that addressed women's needs, understood women's experience, and supported women's struggles. As women who had contributed to a feminist-oriented therapeutic practice in the United States—both as clients and as therapists—we were eager to learn together and share our skills with women where we now lived. Sisters in Great Britain talked about the absolute dearth of therapy services they could use and we felt that a center could help redress this situation in many ways. It could offer psychotherapy from a feminist perspective; it would be a focus for those interested in women's psychology; and it could by its very existence highlight the shortcomings for and biases against women of existing treatment practices in mental hospitals, outpatient psychiatric clinics, analytic institutes, child-guidance clinics, and similar institutions.

Our training as therapists had come out of our involvement in the women's liberation movement and the desire to understand and change the conditions of our lives. We had learned through the women's movement that our internal and external existences were entwined, that the outside world was inside us, and that we needed to struggle on all fronts to produce social change.

During the following five years the Centre moved to larger premises, began to be funded, and engaged in many activities. As the demand for the Centre's services grew, other women joined with us. By 1982 The Women's Therapy Centre had a staff of ten therapists, three administrators, and a sociology student. In addition, it now offers many therapy groups and workshops run by leaders who are not part of the staff. The growth of the Centre has been propelled by the demand for its services, and, faced with a waiting list for both individual and group therapy since 1978, we decided to use some of our resources by sharing what we were learning with other workers in the mental-health field.

Funded by the Equal Opportunities Commission, we set up a ten-week in-service training program for practicing psychotherapists, psychiatric social workers, psychologists, psychiatrists, and counselors. The course meetings consisted of a lecture and discussion group followed by small supervision groups led by us and by our colleague Sally Berry. This book is a refinement and an expansion of the lectures we offered to the participants in those courses. The courses led us to supervise the work of many psychotherapists. In this way we were to hear about the lives and psychologies of scores of women, adding to our experiences with our own clients. In

1981 The Women's Therapy Centre Institute in New York, a sister organization to The Women's Therapy Centre, was set up with our colleague Carol Bloom to extend this kind of training to working psychotherapists in the United States. It is on this practice that we base our analysis of women's psychology.

As full-time members of The Women's Therapy Centre we have given talks and lectures all over Europe and the United States. Everywhere we have gone we have met enthusiastic audiences receptive to the ideas presented in this book. What we were seeing in our clinical practice was confirmed by many therapists who had been working in isolation.

Internally our learning has taken place in three specific ways. One has been the peer supervision group for the staff at The Women's Therapy Centre. Here we have discussed what we were learning about women's psychology from the point of view of practice and technique. The group has shared a feminist perspective, although the routes into feminist psychotherapy were different for all of us and our group has always had some theoretical differences. The second context has been the staff study group, where we have talked extensively without pressure and with great pleasure about our views on such topics as female sexuality, depression, psychological development, and dreams, always trying to start from our own personal and clinical experiences before moving on to reading. The third component of our learning has come from being a part of the office administration—seeing what people want from The Women's Therapy Centre by helping to answer the hundreds of telephone calls and letters that arrive each week from all parts of the country.

The women who have come to The Women's Therapy

Centre have, in their therapy, intimately shared with us parts of themselves. In so doing they have contributed to the creation of a clear and detailed picture of what is going on for all women psychologically within the present conditions of patriarchal social relations. We have found that most current theory and practice of psychotherapy is imprisoned within conventional patriarchal ideology and that women are being poorly served by present psychotherapeutic methods and approaches. The women's movement has now reached a level of development where it is possible to begin to articulate a radically new psychological theory of women based on feminist principles. The outline of a new understanding of the construction of a feminine psychology and the implications this suggests for the practice of feminist psychotherapy are the tasks of this book. The reader will notice that we have included fairly extensive reading notes at the end of each chapter. The content of these varies. Sometimes they are used to provide the historical background to an idea or development; sometimes to expand upon a point that would be disruptive in the main body of the text; sometimes they are simply references. We have placed them at the end of each chapter so that the reader will have easy access to them.

We thank Jo Ann Miller for her thoughtful comments on how to expand this American edition, Linda Carbone for seeing it through the production process, and Joseph Schwartz and Jeremy Pikser for continuing encouragement and enthusiasm for our work. This book owes much to our mothers, Myrna Eichenbaum, Ruth Orbach, and Anne Marie Sandler.

Not only has our clinical practice served as data, so too has our relationship. We have struggled together as two women to develop a loving, equal relationship. This book is a consolidation of our five years at The Women's Therapy Centre in London. It represents the work we have developed, hand in hand, and our love for each other.

New York and London
Summer 1982

UNDERSTANDING
WOMEN

CHAPTER 1

Locating Feminist Psychotherapy: Consciousness-Raising Groups, Object Relations Theory, and Gender Identity

THE women's liberation movement has given us a totally new way to understand women's psychology. As millions of women in the 1960s and 1970s rebelled against an impossible social role, first in one-to-one conversations, then meeting together in consciousness-raising groups, organizations, marches, and protest actions, an understanding of the inner dimensions of women's social position slowly emerged. Women examined their life experiences together and named the system that was oppressing them: patriarchy.

Women in the movement formed consciousness-raising groups in which they uncovered the stories of their lives as women. As they talked, the threads of common experience in the family, at school, with sex, at work, in the medical system, and elsewhere began to knit together a picture of women's lives and women's oppression. Women discovered that they shared feelings of powerlessness and rage, of frustration and underdevelopment, a sense of themselves as less than whole people. They had common experiences of being led into specific roles and activities, of being discriminated against, of being limited in sexual expression and restricted in many other areas of life and growth. The consciousness-raising groups reflected the skills that women have learned well: how to listen and how to talk to each other, how to empathize, how to give emotional support.

In these groups we, along with many others, filled in the pieces of the jigsaw and began to construct a picture of how society educates and molds women into second-class citizenship. We began to see the social basis of our individually experienced oppression. There was always an attempt to understand private lives, individual thoughts, and individual actions from the vantage point of the *fact* of the overall oppression of women.

As the women's liberation movement grew, so did its impact on society. As feminists went into schools and hospitals to change education and medical policy, they joined with sympathizers within those institutions who were raising issues pertinent to the experience of women. Psychology, psychiatry, and psychoanalysis were no less confronted by feminism than were other institutions of patriarchal power. Spearheaded by Phyllis Chesler's illuminating study of women and the mental-health establishment,[1] the Mental Patients Liberation Front, the Radical Therapy Collective in Cambridge, Massachusetts,[2] and the professionals who fought for removal of homosexuality from the category of psychopathological illnesses, the whole mental-health field was turned upside down. Two widely quoted studies, Pauline Bart's "Depression in Middle-Aged Women"[3] and Broverman et al.'s "Sex-Role Stereotypes in Clinical Judgements of Mental Health,"[4] focused on two fundamental issues related to women and mental health. The Bart study discussed the definition of mental health as derived from "feelings of well-being dependent on a positive self-concept" and showed how the internalization of the female role denies women the possibility of a positive self-concept. The Broverman study illustrated how psychology as a discipline and a therapy contributes to maintaining sexist attitudes in the clinical treatment of women. Meanwhile, at the Twenty-ninth International Psychoanalytic Congress, held in London in July 1975, the Freudians' dialogue on Freud and female sexuality in itself demonstrated the impact of the women's liberation movement.[5]

The women's liberation movement provided the theoretical starting point for the development of a feminist theory of women's psychology. The consciousness-raising group was the practical means through which attempts at a feminist psychotherapy began. The present feminist rethinking has emerged from an examination of the psychosocial role of women. What is this social role that has demanded such massive questioning?

Adult women today were brought up in a world in which their primary role was to be wives and mothers, while man's primary role was to be the family breadwinner. Typically, the young woman grows up knowing that she will meet a man who will be her partner in life and that he will hope to look after her economically while she bears children and makes a home. These features of women's social role—growing into a woman (with attendant conditioning), finding a mate, becoming a wife, learning to take care of babies, and making a home involve extensive social preparation. They are not inevitable consequences of women's biology. To find a man, a woman has to present herself in a certain way. She has to develop her sexuality along particular lines; she has to create an image of herself that a man will find pleasing. This is a complex social matter, not at all a straightforward, natural process.

As a girl grows up she takes in the images of the women

around her—mother, grandmother, aunts, teachers, sisters, movie stars, women in books and magazines—consciously and subconsciously forming a future image of herself as a woman. She looks to them as she develops her own sexuality. How she manages her sexuality will be very important, for it is through this aspect of herself that she will find her place in the world. Female sexuality is not simply experienced by the woman as an aspect of herself that she can enjoy and communicate; it is, because of her social position, both a product for herself and her product in the world. Women's sexuality has been a means by which women have found their place, whatever their social class and ethnic background.

In the course of being a wife, the woman will be required to make a home, organize all household matters as smoothly and efficiently as she can, and be a helpmate to her husband, making sure that all the things he needs in his daily life are available—that his meals are cooked, his clothes at the ready, and his social life arranged as he wishes. Being a wife is like having a job, but the training for this job is not overt, nor is the job itself valued. Because the preparation for this job is woven throughout a girl's life it can actually come to *feel* natural. The way she has come to know herself as a person in the world is as a girl and then a woman. Part of being a girl and a woman, as we now know it, means having the skills necessary for being a wife and a mother.

There is still pressure on married women to have children. Being a wife and becoming a mother are so deeply entwined that a woman who has been married for several years and has not had a child senses the curiosity and concern of others about her childlessness and may feel somewhat odd herself.

The woman as mother must *learn* how to take care of

babies, change their diapers, feed them, respond to them emotionally, and help them develop as well-adjusted children into the same social sex roles she grew up with. In the first stages of their lives she will be responsible for arranging appropriate activities for them and structuring the life of the whole family. She will be expected to deal with the emotional realms of family life, keeping contacts with and having knowledge about the various branches of her own and her husband's extended family. Emotions will be her concern.

Women who participated in the women's liberation movement were able to discern a distinct shape to women's lives. They began to see aspects of their day-to-day experiences from an entirely fresh perspective. As a result of the evidence accumulating in consciousness-raising groups it became clear that women have a social existence. It is through women's experience in society that an understanding of their psychology must be sought; not, as it is usually taught, the other way around, whereby women's social roles are seen to flow naturally from women's psychology, a psychology invariably seen as determined by biology. The feminist analysis of women's psychology shows the enormous extent to which their actions and feelings have been concentrated on trying to cope with society's rules about what and who women should be. The development of a new understanding of women's experiences and women's psychology rests on bringing into bold relief exactly what these rules are.

The first psychological demand that flows from a woman's social role is that she must *defer* to others—follow their lead, articulate her needs only in relation to theirs. In essence, she is not to be the main actor in her own life. As a result of this social requirement, women come to believe that they are not important in themselves for themselves. They come to feel unworthy, undeserving, and unentitled. Women are frequently self-deprecating and hesitant about their own initiatives. They are reluctant to speak for themselves, to voice their own thoughts and ideas, to act on their own behalf. Being pushed to defer to others means that they come to undervalue and feel insecure about their wants and their opinions. A woman's recognition of her own needs can therefore be complicated, and a process often occurs in which *women come to hide their desires from themselves.*

The social requirement of deferring may lead a woman to feel as if she is a shadow. A tragic aspect of this individually experienced inequality is that women are isolated in their feelings of inadequacy and lack of confidence. They cannot imagine that other women have similar feelings. This painful comparison further isolates a woman and leaves her with bad feelings about herself. She may imagine that other women's lives are more fulfilling and wonder how they achieve that fulfillment.

The second requirement of woman's social role is that she must always be *connected* to others and shape her life in accordance with a man's. A woman's status will derive from that of her mate. Indeed, her very sense of self and well-being may rely on her connection with him. A woman may look to a man to complete her life, to give her an identity and a purpose. Women come to feel odd, not right within themselves, if they are not connected to a man. Our culture does not have a positive image of a woman on her own. Singleness is never seen as a choice, but as something that befalls her and engenders sympathy. The word for a single woman is *spinster.* It conjures up ghastly images of coldness, sadness, and deprivation. (*Bachelor* suggests excitement and freedom.) Self-containment and separateness feel selfish, self-centered, and even aggressive for a woman. They are out of the ordinary and somewhat frightening. Since connection to others must be maintained, a woman must make herself into a person others will find pleasing; in making herself in their image she may end up not knowing who she is. *She loses herself.*

The requirements of being connected to others and of deferring to them lead to another psychological concomitant of woman's social role: that of having *emotional antennae.* A woman must learn to anticipate others' needs. The vulnerable and helpless infant who has no language needs a caregiver to intuit unspoken messages and communications. A girl's life involves preparation for this skill, and once acquired it is part of her psychology and it is brought to all relationships. The woman handles the emotional reins. This will be no less true in a job situation, where her emotional strengths will often be called upon. She must care for others and help them to express what they need, particularly at the emotional level. Once she has understood what others need, she must help them satisfy those needs. Part of her social role as caregiver and nurturer of others involves putting her own needs second. Yet her needs do not remain merely secondary but often become hidden, for she herself does not have an emotional caregiver to turn to. There is an imbalance in the giving. *A woman then carries deep feelings of neediness.*

The intricacy of woman's psychosocial role is woven into the family in the relationship that will have the most profound bearing on her psychological development. The girl learns her social role from her mother, as her mother did from her own mother. The girl's personality, her psychology, takes shape through her relationship with her mother. The daughter spends most of her early life with mother, who is responsible for child-rearing. Mother and daughter share a gender and social-role identification.

The importance of the mother to the daughter's psychology has come to prominence over the past several years. New lines of development do not emerge in isolation. Authors like Nancy Chodorow, Nancy Friday, Adrienne Rich, Signe Hammer, Luce Irigay, and Elena Giannini Belotti[6] have begun to explore the meaning and impact of the mother-daughter relationship. Groups focusing on this relationship have flourished. Such investigations allow us to uncover the crucial impact of this relationship in the developing girl's sense of self, especially in the very earliest years of life.

While father is a very important person in the girl's world, he is rarely the center of it during the first two years of her life. In fact, father is strikingly absent. Time with father may consist of an hour at night, five minutes in the morning. Under these circumstances time with father may be experienced as pleasurable, exciting, or perhaps a little frightening. Father may be adored or feared or somewhere in between. But however he is experienced by the daughter, he is special, exotic; he does not inhabit the girl's world on a regular basis. Important for girls' psychological development is the fact that *father is constantly leaving;* he does not stay and share in the girl's world of mother and children. (Siblings, who are outside the primary orbit, are nevertheless part of the world of home.) When father enters their orbit the nuances of the primary communication change, for he represents and is in his presence someone from outside. He brings with him his experience and an aura of the world outside the home; he symbolizes maleness, worldliness, and separateness. Thus girls grow up with a preconscious knowledge of the limited contact they will have with men.

In focusing on the tremendous impact that family structure and relationships have on girls' development, we and many other women found ourselves looking to psychotherapy and psychology as a detailed way of thinking about the construction of femininity and as an extension of the consciousness-raising process. After a few years of consciousness-raising groups and public political activity outside the groups, because profound changes had taken place, we began to perceive the limitations of the consciousness-raising groups. We found ourselves in a situation in which consciousness was changing tremendously fast, and so was the pattern of women's lives in terms of their relationships at home, at work, and with their children and families, but in which society as a whole was not keeping pace with the kinds of changes women were demanding. Women felt that they had changed a lot and yet society had not: material changes did not reflect changes in consciousness. Because society was not altering radically enough to consolidate the changes in consciousness, we found that many aspects of our behavior, instead of being continually challenged and reshaped, seemed to stand still. Changing our own behavior and feelings was also sometimes excruciatingly difficult. We believed that women should now feel assertive and entitled; we believed women should be independent, not possessive or insecure; but these beliefs did not lead to habitual emotional responses. For example, a woman could be pleased to be presenting a paper at a conference but might be filled with anxiety at being heard and being so visible.

A second difficulty, which we can analyze in retrospect, was that precisely because the consciousness-raising groups were so emotionally charged—everything was so new, exciting, and frightening—feelings between members in the groups were often not handled very well. Feelings of envy, competition, anger, and love emerged and were so powerful that the groups sometimes could not cope with them. Women in these groups had to ask: How do we change what is so deeply rooted in us? How can I change how I feel? How can I understand what is going on at an unconscious level?

Through the process of trying to change our society we

had made ourselves more conscious and had begun to understand how social expectations were affecting us on a psychological level. We continued to feel unentitled, unexperienced, or unequal. We discovered how we felt about the obligations and restrictions we experienced on a daily basis. This discovery on a feeling level led us to try to discover the vital connections between the social world that women inhabit and the inner private world that governs us in the deepest reaches of our personalities.[7] We, together with many women, found ourselves looking to psychotherapy to see if it could give us access to some of these answers.

The study of psychoanalysis proved problematic for many feminists at this time, because of the anti-Freud bias of some sections of the movement.[8] Freudian psychoanalytic practice was seen to be explicitly reactionary in relation to its understandings of women's psychology and femininity.[9] Some feminists believed psychoanalysis did have something to offer, but at that time they were in the minority.[10] Many women were drawn to "humanistic" psychology, the growth-movement psychotherapies, which seemed to offer a way to discover parts of themselves that were repressed, split off, or in opposition to the stereotyped view they held of themselves.[11] The techniques of Gestalt therapy, transactional analysis, psychodrama, assertion training, and other such therapies were accessible and could be learned fairly quickly. These therapeutic techniques offered three advantages: first, they held the possibility that people could get in touch with their feelings more speedily than through psychoanalytic methods; second, they encouraged individuals to act on their own behalf; and third, they demystified the process of psychological change.

After several years of practice based on these tenets, outstanding innovations were introduced, mostly in the context of group therapy.[12] Theme-centered groups on assertiveness training, compulsive eating, anger, and sexuality were developed. Women were feeling and being more assertive, getting in touch with a range of emotions previously defined as taboo for women, and feeling and acting differently in the world. They were able to know more clearly what they felt and to speak up for themselves at work, at home, in the course of daily situations. However, persistent stumbling blocks to emotional change led us to give more attention to unconscious processes, and to the serious study of psychoanalytic, psychotherapeutic practice. The turn to psychoanalysis came from our new understanding of the importance of early family experience in forming our psychology. At that time, humanistic psychology, working in the here and now, seemed to limit the satisfactory exploration of family history and the unconscious. Many feminists were already using certain psychoanalytic tools in their work and incorporating them into psychotherapeutic practice. Interpretations were made about transference in the discussion of family history, in the therapy relationship, and encouragement was given for analyzing and discussing dreams in therapy. In turning to psychoanalysis, we were interested in three specific areas. We recognized the importance of Freud's discovery of the unconscious; we were trying to understand the vicissitudes of a psychic life that was a powerful determinant in the politics of everyday experience; and we wanted to understand girls' psychological development.

Within psychoanalysis we were drawn to what is loosely called the British Object Relations School, and especially the work of Fairbairn, Winnicott, and Guntrip,[13] for two reasons. First, the clinical descriptions of Winnicott's and Guntrip's[14] work in particular echoed with much of what we were seeing in our clinical practices. Their observations about what the individual wants and needs in terms of contact and care in therapy confirmed our own experience of our women clients. Second, their understanding about the construction of personality was based firmly within a relational context. As feminists, we saw the connection between individual experience, personality, and the material world. We saw the content of the unconscious as an intrapsychic reflection of the impact of present child-rearing and gender arrangements. The object-relations approach was therefore consonant with our own. It posited a materialist view of psychological development on the basis that the individual has a need for relationship and a drive for contact with another human being, and that the first two years of life are the most important time for the development of the inner core of the person, the psyche and the personality together, which Fairbairn and Guntrip mean when they refer to the ego.[15] What they observed and what we shall be referring to is a model of psychological development in which what happens outside the womb, and in earliest relationships, is primary. We shall be talking mainly about the mother-child relationship because our culture has women mothering and for the most part being sole child rearers and caregivers for infants and young children.

What makes each person unique is the particular way in which each personality—each person's ego—is formed. Ego development begins at birth, and the food for the developing psyche is contact in a human relationship. The infant has a *primary* need for human contact. Without such contact babies fail to thrive and even die.[16] From the moment of birth, babies enter a social world; they do not yet have fully developed personalities, of course, but they have the capacity to become a part of human culture. All their subsequent experiences of physical and emotional growth are part of the process of becoming a person in a particular social context. The first month of a baby's life seems to be a continuation of life within the uterus. The infant apparently still lives in an enclosed world, preoccupied with physical needs for food, warmth, and physical contact. But the baby is in fact floating in a world of new sounds, smells, and tactile stimulation, and from the sixth week on we begin to see the infants' active responses to the stimuli. Their eyes focus and connect with people around them. They begin to explore themselves and their environment in new ways. They touch their toes and hands, their mothers' breasts, other people's hands, as if to grasp the objects that inhabit their world. Now babies are experiencing themselves and the mother as being within the same physical and psychological world inside a common boundary. Still, they do not yet have a sense of themselves as defined, separate persons.

In the first months of life the mothering person is the most constant person in the infant's world. She is the anchor, the mediator for the baby's experiences.[17] The baby relies for survival on the mother's empathy, attentiveness, and understanding, and a sort of psychological umbilical cord ties them together. This invisible connection of emotion experienced and transmitted from adult to infant feeds the developing psyche of the infant. This is not to say that the baby is an empty receptacle waiting to be filled, but rather that there is an intricate process in which the caring environment responds to the baby's needs. Babies are very expressive before the acquisition of language. Through a range of cries, noises, and facial expressions they communicate to those around them. A baby's communications and the responses to them are necessary and important aspects of the process of development. It is through these communications that babies make their needs known.

The caring, love, attention, and security the mother provides are all experienced and taken in by the infant. Part of the appropriate empathy and nurturance is the ability of the caregiver to provide a structure, a containment, and a sense of boundaries for the baby. All during this early period the mother is empathizing with the baby's needs. Because the baby is in the process of developing a sense of self and does not yet have any boundaries, the mother must bring the boundaries into the relationship; she must relate to the baby as a separate person. Responding appropriately, which at times includes saying *no* and setting limits, provides a safety net and a sense of containment for the baby.

When secure ego development occurs, we see the baby beginning to maintain a sense of self even when its caregiver is not present. The baby now embodies the love and care of the other. Mother is no longer the only person with a sense of self within this relationship. This means that babies do not experience a loss of self when mother leaves the room.[18] They experience, with varying degrees of upset and acceptance, the temporary loss of mother, but recover their equilibrium readily. The baby has some sense of self apart from, *separate from,* mother. The experience of continued love and caring is critical to this sense of security within the baby. Secure in the love of its caregiver, the infant feels that mother will return and the caring will continue. The love is an invisible thread between baby and mother, so that although they are physically apart there remains a reliable connection between them.

Achieving a clear sense of psychological separation is extremely problematic. We know that in the first two years all babies are bound to have frustrating and upsetting experiences as well as nurturing ones. In an ideal situation the caregiver needs to be able to convey that the infant will survive such experiences, and able to accept and contain the infant's upset so that the connection can be relied upon.

Frustrating or upsetting experiences need not be caused by inadequate caring or attention. For an infant the experience of hunger, even if it is only for two or three minutes, can be distressing. A baby's upset does not necessarily signify mother's withholding or lack of caring. The infant's experience of feeling hunger and then expressing distress is a necessary communication from the baby to the world. The response to this kind of communication is important because it shows the baby what kind of impact it has on its environment. In so far as needs are responded to and frustrations are accepted and tolerated, the caregiver is connecting and relating with the baby and, consequently, temporary separation is more likely to be possible. When the caregiver has difficulty in connecting and relating to the baby, the absence of connection makes the process of separation by baby less likely. When secure development does not occur, the process of separation is modified. Babies may feel insecure in the world and not experience a separate identity. To the extent that their needs for contact go unmet, infants are not able to achieve psychological separation because they are still yearning and still in need of the psychological umbilical cord with mother. These babies have not had sufficient nurturance or containment to stand separate.

However the mother responds, a crucial factor is that the baby experiences her or his upset in relation to mother. This is of enormous importance in the developing psychology of the infant and later the child. Thus the image of mother in each person's internal world is extremely powerful. Mother is embedded psychically in almost magical terms.[19]

The developing infant is, at a certain level, helpless. Babies' communications will not always be understood and they cannot control the actions of the caregiver. On the psychological and physical levels they are utterly vulnerable and dependent. Although the infant is in this sense passive, there is enormous activity of an internal nature. The embryonic psyche takes the only path available and transfers the difficult situation to the world of inner reality, where it can exercise more control. In other words, there is at the same moment an internal experience of an "outside" situation. The external situation may be completely out of the infant's control and therefore not alterable, but the internal experience is malleable and adjustable. In the baby's internal world he or she juggles relationships so that they provide more satisfaction. In this sense infants have an *internal* life, of involving relationships. Because these relationships are stripped of their truly interactive nature they are essentially relations with *objects*.

This dynamic of taking something into the inner world can be understood, if we think of the way in which we, as adults, try to cope with upsetting situations by replaying and rearranging them in our heads. We imagine the situation in a different, more satisfactory way in our daydreams and come up with creative solutions. So it is for the child. During this early process of development, the infant is internalizing the unacknowledged distressing experience and attempting to change it. But alas, this attempt fails. The inner world is always interacting with the outside world, with real people. The internal construction of object relations is thus modified by these actual experiences. The unsatisfying experiences that occur in relation to mother then find their expressions in a particular reflection of her in the infant's inner world. Mother becomes a disappointing person who has to be split in two: the known and longed-for giving mother and the known and deeply disappointing mother. In the inner economy of the infant's embryonic psyche, the unsatisfying object continues to frustrate her or his needs at the same time that it whets them with the potential of satisfaction. In the external world, however, if the needs continue to be unmet, the infant gets hungrier and hungrier for what is wanted and needed. The outside world appears less nourishing.

A client named Ruth gives us a good illustration of how these experiences appear in the psychology of adults. Ruth has had some good experiences with her mother throughout her life. However, her mother has a great deal of difficulty in giving warmth and love and often appears as a cold, ungiving, teasing person. Because Ruth has not received sufficient nurturance she is unable to achieve a psychological separation from her mother. She still feels entwined with her and in need of her in essential ways.

Ruth now copes with the disappointing and upsetting experiences with her mother by controlling them and "forgetting" the pain of her unmet needs. She tries to transform the image of her mother, because acceptance of the reality is too painful. The unconscious processes began with Ruth taking into herself, very early in her psychological development, the frustrating experiences with her mother. She has repressed and, in her psyche, divided this unsatisfying mother (object) into two. One part, which is unresponsive, continually disappoints her and makes her feel rejected. Each time Ruth visits her mother she is hoping on an unconscious level that this time mother will be the warm, loving mother Ruth needs and wants. Ruth craves her mother's acceptance so that she can finally feel good within herself and become a separate person. But inevitably the visits are painful. Ruth feels disappointed and unsatisfied. Ruth's inner world is in ascendancy and she cannot tolerate the fact that mother is cold and ungiving. Thus she again makes mother potentially satisfying, and the internal split of mother is perpetuated. At a conscious level Ruth feels mother should, could, be doing more. She still wants so much and feels bad for the wanting.

Set against such difficulties in early relating are the more positive experiences that are the threads which weave good connections between infant and caregiver and the development of a secure psychology. Consistent love, appropriate nurturance, and the setting of boundaries create a sense of psychological well-being. These experiences promote a positive sense of self, self-love, internal substance, and a feeling that the world is basically safe.

The existential phenomenon of realizing oneself as a separate person, as a subject in the world, comes about through a process of secure, positive development. Through the baby's earlier interactions and the "taking in" of others relating to it, the baby develops a self and a personality. The infant embodies the love, care, and security of those around it and comes to feel visible and substantive. In the period from six to eighteen months the sense of mother and others as "other"—as external people—develops. Communications and responses to the baby all contribute to the weaving process that produces the psychological birth of a person.[20] In the early months, therefore, the mother allows the infant to be totally connected, merged. Then, being in tune with the baby's changing needs, the mother lets go to some degree as the baby begins to separate and become his or her own person. During this process, called separation-individuation, children are continually establishing a clearer sense of themselves. They begin to test their own independence. The child's future sense of adventure, curiosity, and taste for life are strongly affected by the attitudes, conscious and unconscious, of the people around her or him at this time.

The earlier experience of life—that of being merged with

mother, of the world and baby all being one—now changes
and there is, for the baby, an outside and a sense of "I."
Infants begin to experience their own existence. They now
explore their fingers and toes in a new way. There is a new
curiosity as baby touches and looks at the faces of others.

Father's presence is also reflected in the developing personality of the baby. Fathers for the most part have less interaction with small infants, being somewhere outside the
orbit of mother and infant. Before the process of separation
the father may be experienced within the infant's world, but
it is the mother who is the consistent presence. Father is
with the infant far less and so his smell, touch, and sound are
not the familiar ones of mother. Just as father experiences his
wife and himself as the couple and the baby as the third
person in a triangle, the baby experiences herself or himself
with mother and may feel father to be the third person, the
outsider.

As babies develop, realize their separateness, and become
aware of the people and things around them, they now look
to father with new curiosity, trying to take in a sense of this
very different person. This often occurs much earlier than in
the past, now that some fathers are consciously involved in
child rearing, either as part of a nuclear family or in innova-
tive familial arrangements. The father plays an important
part in the baby's attempt to separate from mother. For the
baby boy, father is "other" than mother and like him. The
boy identifies with father and uses him to separate himself
further from mother. He may emulate and imitate father as
the role model for the person he is to become.

For the little girl, father is "other," whereas the little boy
experiences himself as "other" from the moment of birth
because mother relates to him as "other." The little girl,
being of the same gender as mother, has not experienced

intimacy with an "other." Her original intimacy is homosexual. Feeling herself to be the "other" with father aids the little girl in her developing sense of separateness.[21] She can feel boundaries with father that she may not feel with mother.

For both girl and boy infants the relationship with father—the quality of his caring, loving, withholding, and distancing—will play an important part in their developing psyches. An older brother may also serve as an "other" for the little girl, and she may move close to the brother in her attempts to separate from mother. However it is directed, the sense of "otherness" based upon sexual differences is central to psychological development.

As babies move toward their psychological birth as separate persons, they learn that people fall into two categories, female and male. By the age of one, children can point to male and female figures as either mom or dad and at eighteen months they can recognize themselves as either female or male.[22]

The baby's developing personality is highly influenced by this early sense of gender identity and the assimilation of either a feminine or a masculine gender. From the time an infant is born the family assigns it a place and role in the world based in large part upon its sex. In the most minor and major ways every communication and contact with the baby is imbued with a sense of gender and with the profoundly different expectations for girls and boys which the parents and others have and which the child learns. In all cultures one of the primary laws is that of sexual categories of masculine and feminine. People are not seen to be simply human, or even human with differing sexual and biological characteristics of masculinity and femininity. In our culture, as in many other cultures, these characteristics are not equal.[23]

For instance, "strong," "rugged," "capable," and "confident" are examples of valued masculine characterizations, while "petite," "delicate," "helpless," "giving," "pretty," "dainty," and "demure" are prized feminine ones. Infants, then, are anticipated in gender categories. Will it be a boy? Is it a girl? All those who relate to a baby will have specific expectations for a girl and for a boy.

Before the emergence of the women's movement, it was widely believed that women's psychology derived from their biology—that is, their reproductive function—and men's psychology from theirs. Only recently have attempts been made to separate the biological, psychological, and cultural aspects of personality development. New studies of gender identity show that by the time a child is two years old this identity is firmly fixed. These studies are a direct challenge to previous views in psychoanalysis. For Freud a child was bisexual for the first years of life, and at the oedipal phase (age four or five) came to know itself as feminine or masculine. (See note 9.) On the other hand, the post-Freudian view of psychosexual development posited that human beings are born with masculine or feminine sexuality. Both positions are based, at bottom, on the belief that biological sex determines masculinity or femininity. Research in the area of gender identity, then, has been of particular interest to feminists, for its findings are a direct challenge to the idea that biology determines psychology.

Money and Erhardt, psychologists who have studied people with mixed sexual characteristics, argue that to understand concepts of masculinity and femininity we must separate the biological basis from the cultural.[24] Their work shows very clearly that the ideas we hold about femininity and masculinity relate to the cultural practices of a given society and not to biological imperatives. Human beings are not born with a masculine or a feminine psychology; rather, women's and men's psychologies are fashioned to fit in with what is thought of as masculine and feminine. These researchers argue that apart from biological sex—women's capacity to menstruate, conceive, give birth, and lactate—and men's capacity to impregnate, the attributes we associate with femininity and masculinity are cultural constructions.

Money and Erhardt found that hermaphrodites who are brought up as females, despite the lack of ovaries and even with the development of male secondary sexual characteristics, continued to see themselves as females, and organized their world view within feminine perspectives based on gender assignment. When these hermaphrodites discovered secondary sexual characteristics of the opposite sex, this did not create gender-identity confusion, but a desire to erase the opposite-sex manifestations. Hermaphrodites raised as males were equally determined to remain male. If biology were at the root of masculinity and femininity, these individuals would have suffered a severe gender-identity crisis. Instead, they were very eager to maintain themselves as women or as men, and to get rid of any physical characteristics that did not relate to their gender.

Along with this knowledge of oneself as a girl or a boy goes, as we know, a series of behaviors, feelings, and actions that are deemed appropriate for each sex. The stereotyping of sex roles means that boys and girls feel uncomfortable, awkward, and out of place if they are involved in activities that have been presented to them as out of bounds for their sex. Although sex-role stereotyping is universal, it varies from culture to culture, and the rigidity of each child's immediate environment varies. As a result many girls grow up with the idea that it is perfectly acceptable for women to become engineers, to be assertive, or not to be linked to a mate, while other women's sexual identity would be threatened if they were to perform typically masculine tasks or follow a "bachelor" life style. But however varied the child's environment, some activities are seen as definitely outside the child's and later the adult's realm because of his or her sex. They will feel wrong. *The construction of personality is always linked to a person's sense of gender identity.*

This is an extremely important starting point for us and for a feminist-oriented women's psychology, not only because it sweeps away the cobwebs of biological determinism but also for the light it sheds on the importance of social experience in human life, particularly in infancy and childhood. In contrast to the views of many psychologists, we stress the importance of culture in shaping the needs, desires, and psychic life of both women and men, so that *femininity and masculinity are psychological entities within a social context.* Gender identity and a sense of self emerge together and reflect the prevailing culture and pattern of parenting. It is within this context that we ask the question: What is a feminine psychology and how is it constructed?

Notes

1. Phyllis Chesler, *Women and Madness,* New York, 1972.

2. See Phil Brown, ed., *Radical Psychology,* New York, 1973; Jerome Angel, *The Radical Therapist,* New York, 1971.

3. Pauline Bart, "Depression in Middle-Aged Women," in V. Gornick and B. K. Moran, eds., *Women in Sexist Society,* New York, 1971.

4. I. K. Broverman, D. M. Broverman, F. E. Clarkson, P. S. Rosenkrantz, and S. R. Vogel, "Sex-Role Stereotypes in Clinical Judgements of Mental Health," *Journal of Consulting and Clinical Psychology* 34 (1970) 1–7.

5. See *International Journal of Psycho-analysis* 57 (1976).

6. See N. Chodorow, *The Reproduction of Mothering,* Berkeley, 1978; N.

Friday, *My Mother, My Self,* New York, 1977; A. Rich, *Of Woman Born,* New York, 1976; S. Hammer, *Daughters and Mothers, Mothers and Daughters,* New York, 1975; L. Irigay in *Signs,* Vol 7, No. 1 (Autumn 1981), and Elena Giannini Belotti, *Little Girls,* London, 1975.

7. There are four major links between the consciousness-raising process and feminist psychotherapy. The first of these is that the women's liberation movement asserted that personal life is a political affair. This was, of course, a direct challenge to the progressive left-wing movements of the 1960s, which saw concern with personal matters as individualistic. Within the consciousness-raising group each person's experience, each woman's life story, was a matter of interest. We understood that through listening to an individual's experience we could draw a much richer picture of how society is put together. Sexual politics provided an understanding of how society works both at an ideological level and at a material level, and deepened the understanding the left had of human experience. The women's movement built an analysis of society founded on the nuts and bolts of individual life experience. It enlarged and challenged previous understanding of the social, economic, and political bases of society.

The psychotherapy process is similarly concerned with the details of individual experience. Through in-depth analysis of an individual's conscious and unconscious life, psychoanalytic psychotherapists have theorized about the workings of society, for the investigation of a person's psyche reveals the ensemble of social relations.

The second link between the consciousness-raising group and psychotherapy is the focus on the family. The mythical family, still portrayed by the media as the norm, is one in which father is the breadwinner and works outside the home and mother works contentedly inside the home, raising the children, smoothly oiling the wheels of domesticity, and providing emotional nurturing. Even if our own family did not fit this image (for example, if one parent was absent, or father was not the breadwinner, or both parents worked outside the home), it was nevertheless organized on sexual lines, with women and men having clearly defined roles and responsibilities. In the consciousness-raising group and in psychotherapy we discover the importance of the family in shaping our own childhoods and in determining our experience of becoming adult. We focus on relationships within the family and the expectations, affections, rewards, and restrictions that influence our behavior and attitudes as little girls and subsequently as women.

The family is our first social world. In it we first learn our sexual roles. Feminists have taken up the history of the family and shown how, in its present form, it is a recent development. The transformation from a feudal economy to a modern capitalist state has gone hand in hand with changes in the family unit which have led to the sexual division of labor within the family and the relegation of women to subordinate positions as wives and mothers. A feminist psychotherapy is interested in how the social practices of a given culture are transmitted to its members and how the individual internalizes the power relations, sex roles, and psychodynamics of the family.

The third link between consciousness raising and psychotherapy is that both processes are concerned with the emotional life of the individual. In the consciousness-raising group women came to feel more comfortable with and less ashamed of the strong feelings they were beginning to discover inside themselves. Anger, pain, depression, and sadness were seen as understandable expressions of a woman's psychological experience. This kind of discovering and untapping of taboo emotions is very much a part of the psychotherapeutic process. Given the basic principle of the validity of emotional life, both consciousness-raising and psychotherapy look beyond the content and construction of particular emotions; for example, romantic or passionate feelings are not taken at face value but are scrutinized for clues to understanding their derivation and grasping why such feelings are so important in the individual and collective lives of women.

The fourth link centers on the topic of sexuality, previously a taboo subject. From Freud onward psychotherapists have been engaged in the study of sexuality at an emotional, philosophical, and political level. In consciousness-raising groups women began to try to understand what sexuality is—how it is formed, what it means in our lives, what kinds of dissatisfactions (and satisfactions) we have, whether sexuality is something sacred, and whether sexual relationships are in some sense also political relationships. We tried to understand women's sexual fantasies, and that in turn shed light on women's sexual experience. In addition consciousness-raising groups discussed heterosexuality and lesbianism, and not only produced a critique of a heterosexual society but focused on the politics of sexuality.

8. A bias that had progressive elements at the time, particularly in view of the intellectual climate of the United States in the late 1950s. See especially Betty Friedan, *The Feminine Mystique* (1963), for what Freudianism had come to mean about women's psychology in that period.

9. Psychoanalysis has evolved from a treatment for mental distress to a developmental theory of the workings of the human psyche. At the very center of his theory of psychological development Freud placed libido—the human being's struggle to come to terms with her or his sexuality and life energy. Freud asserted that the force of libido could be seen in every aspect of human activity as people repressed and sublimated it. Libido always sought satisfaction, and it was the harnessing of libidinous desires that led to the creation of civilization as we know it. In psychic terms, mental functioning depended on the individual's capacity to repress and express her or his sexuality according to the cultural norm.

Freud gathered the data for his theory through the process of psychoanalysis. By analyzing distress symptoms and exploring the unconscious material of his patients through free association, slips of the tongue, and dreams, he built a theory of psychological development. Freud saw mental life going through a series of stages—oral, anal, and genital—from birth onward, culminating in the oedipal phase at age four or five.

At each developmental stage the libido centered on a different part of the body; it could become fixated at any one of the stages, resulting in psychopathology. Freud saw all individual psychopathology as being on a continuum, with neurotic patterns arising as a result of libidinal arrest at a particular stage. The aim of psychotherapy was to unravel the points of libidinal arrest so that the individual's personality could move on through the remaining developmental stages.

Freud saw the Oedipus complex as the apex of developmental stages, for it was during this stage that the libidinal drive must become fixed in its appropriate heterosexual path. The little boy and the little girl must separate from their attachment to mother in order to take their place in the world. The boy must detach his sexual feelings toward mother so that he can later reattach his sexual feelings to another woman. This detachment occurs as follows: The boy sees his father as a rival for mother's love and wishes to replace him. He wishes to castrate his father and take his place. As a result of this wish or fantasy, the little boy fears retaliation by his father; he fears castration. Fear of his own castration leads him to give up his sexual attachment to his mother by repressing or denying his sexual feelings for her. He then can take his place next to his father, and later on he will have his own woman. For the girl, resolution of the Oedipus complex and separation from mother comes about as follows: At around age three the little girl realizes that she does not have a penis; she immediately thinks she has been castrated and feels the lack. The little girl feels contempt for her mother, who does not have a penis, and blames the mother for her own castration. The little girl's contempt and anger lead her to turn away from her mother and to attach herself to father, who has a penis and might provide her with one. She then gives up her wish for a penis and puts in place of it a wish for a child, and with that purpose in view, she takes her father as a love object.

Concepts such as penis envy, the castration complex, and the Oedipus complex, although first introduced as part of the psychoanalytic dialogue, are now common parlance and have become ideological foundation stones upon which theories of female sexuality and female psychology are built. Freud described a feminine experience that he heard about and saw in his clinical practice. The events, feelings, and nuances he observed have provided subsequent generations with much useful material. However, Freud's observations about women's psychology and femininity were made through patriarchal spectacles. He was either unconscious of or unconcerned about his patriarchal bias, thus the theory he drew from his clinical data suffers from a particular vision. Further, having constructed a theory of female sexuality, he then superimposed it onto the clinical material. Subsequent Freudian analysts who have written about the psychology of women have consistently maintained this bias, although they have revised the theory in other ways.

In common with many other feminists we have several criticisms of Freud and the post-Freudian view of women's psychology. They all stem from a bias that sees female sexuality as tied to reproduction and the gratification of male sexual impulses toward women, to women's inferiority because women and men are different, and to the control and subjugation of women. As such, the theories propose a female sexuality formed within a male image and with reference to the penis. For example, few analysts have discussed the meaning in a

Locating Feminist Psychotherapy

girl's life of her experience of her mother's body as a positive force, or of men's envy of the female body, the body from which they were born. (Had Freud written at a different time, he might have developed a theory according to which the main focus in the psychological development of both boys and girls was on the mother's breasts, the hopes that a girl would have that she would then grow up to have a mother's body, and the boy's feelings of inadequacy because he did not possess those marvelous breasts. After all, babies have far more contact with breasts than with penises.) The Freudian view of how women's psychology develops is fitted into a schema that sees female genitalia and femininity as inadequate and yet inevitable. The issue of female inadequacy, which is a starting point for Freudian theory on femininity, flows from his patriarchal bias.

The consequence of being raised as a daughter in a patriarchal society is that women see themselves as inferior. This sense of inferiority is not formed at the oedipal stage when the girl realizes she is not a boy; it is intimately linked to the very beginning of a girl's life and the acquisition of her gender identity. This sense of gender is woven into the very fabric of earliest experience: infants are related to as girls or as boys with all that attends those terms. When a woman reveals that she feels unsatisfied, inadequate, and empty she is talking about her internal experience of being a woman in our society. These feelings arise because the psychic sphere reflects the fact that she is a woman in a patriarchal culture and thus a second-class citizen.

10. Jean Strouse put together an excellent collection of articles on psychoanalysis which illuminated the areas in which psychoanalytic theory and practice could be extremely useful for an understanding of women's psychology. See Jean Strouse, ed., *Women and Analysis,* New York, 1974. Other psychoanalytic research that feminists were drawn to in the early 1970s included the early work of Wilhelm Reich, the first psychoanalyst to relate individual psychology to the world in which we live in an explicitly political way. In *The Sexual Revolution* he drew on Engels's analysis of the family to discuss the way the family creates a particular psychology. He demonstrated its economic function (as the protector of women and children deprived of economic and sexual rights), and its political function (as a training ground for bourgeois social relations in which the father is "the exponent and representative of the authority of the State in the family"). Reich pointed to the psychic consequences of such an arrangement and to the psychological impact of the economic subservience of women and children on female sexuality. He delineated a line of investigation that was to draw the connections between character structure and economic and social relations. His early work in both the practice and the theory of psychology has been a tremendous inspiration to psychotherapists interested in relating the social and psychological worlds.

Other feminists were drawn to the work of Karen Horney, Clara Thompson, Harry Stack Sullivan, and Erich Fromm, all of them generally associated with the American or Cultural school of psychoanalysis. Drawing on the work of anthropologists and referring to the social conditions of the times in which they worked, Horney and Thompson in particular attempted a sociological analysis

29

of Freud's findings on femininity and stressed the impact of the social world on the individual's psychic structure. But they were less concerned with intrapsychic internalization of the outside world than with the impact of prevailing social attitudes on the formation of personality. For example, they looked at other cultures and saw that although women's social position is subordinate in all of them, the range of activities and experiences open to women differs from culture to culture. From this evidence they were able to argue that femininity and masculinity are constructions intimately related to particular cultures. Although they understood the impact of cultural and social forces on child rearing, they did not dissect the psychodynamics by which the outside world becomes transformed in its particular form in the individual psyche.

Karen Horney tried to develop a theory of women's psychology. She pointed out that women are concerned with power and suggested that this rather than the libido was their motivating force, and that the issues that arise in the female unconscious center on women's lack of power. She also focused attention on how men may suffer from womb envy. Clara Thompson focused on penis envy as symbolic of women's desire for men's power and stated that women were entitled to power in the world and that there was nothing particularly healthy about a woman accepting her lot in life—concepts which were unheard of at the time.

The writings of Horney and Thompson are both accessible and exciting to read. They were revolutionaries within the psychoanalytic community, and they were the first people to bring a feminist perspective into psychoanalysis. Their weakness, from our point of view as working therapists, is that they were not able to explain the particularities of female psychology. Nevertheless, they did break new ground by offering a woman-oriented perspective on women's psychology.

The work of Jacques Lacan has been taken up by European feminist theorists. The most influential of the Lacanian ideas are presented in Juliet Mitchell's *Psychoanalysis and Feminism,* New York, 1974. Mitchell's reading of Freud, after Lacan, provides a richer understanding of feelings of inadequacy at the oedipal stage. She discusses how the girl's discovery of the anatomical differences between the sexes forces her to come to grips with the fact that she cannot win her mother's love as her father does. According to Mitchell, the girl's lack of a penis comes to mean for her not only that she must accept the loss of her first love, but also that her *active* loving is implicated in the defeat. The girl comes to see herself, her mother, and thus all women as damaged and inferior. Aware of her inferior position, she turns to father and attempts to woo him. Mitchell's account parallels Freud's in stating that boys and girls learn their place in the world in relation to their father in the oedipal phase. She explains patriarchy with the theory that boys learn that one day they will become the father, whereas girls learn both that they are rejected by the mother and that they will never take the father's place. Juliet Mitchell has grappled with Freudian theory and expanded it in a creative way. Her major contribution has been to discuss the whole concept of passivity and activity. She puts forward the idea that a girl has to learn passivity and give up an active pursuit of a relationship. In addition, she focuses attention on the daughter's relationship with the mother and on the loss of the mother in the girl's life.

However, neither Freud's nor Mitchell's explanation conforms to our experience in our clinical practice. We have found no evidence that the way women experience themselves as incomplete or inadequate connects in any way with the fantasy of a penis or its transformation into a baby. Furthermore, we believe that femininity is part of a girl's experience from birth and not something that comes about at the oedipal stage. We are not persuaded that instinctual drives of libido and aggression shape human psychology.

11. See, for example, Hogie Wycoff, *Solving Women's Problems,* New York, 1977.

12. See, for example, Susie Orbach, *Fat Is a Feminist Issue,* New York, 1978; Susie Orbach, *Fat Is a Feminist Issue II,* New York, 1982; and Sheila Ernst and Lucy Goodison, *In Our Own Hands,* New York, 1981. Teresa Bernardez-Bonesatti, a feminist psychiatrist, makes a provocative point when, in a study of sixty women, she discusses the developmental levels of feminist and nonfeminist women seeking psychotherapy. She argues that the experience of consciousness raising has enabled feminist women to express their anger and move toward separation-individuation. See *Heresies,* No. 2, May 1977.

13. The work of the British school of Object Relations developed in the 1930s with Melanie Klein's rethinking of psychoanalytic theory based on her analysis of young children. While Klein maintained the stress on instinctual forces, and in particular the death instinct in the organization of psychic life, her detailed examination of the fantasy and play of children provided a richer interpretation of Freudian theory. Focusing her attention on the first years of life, she described the inner world of the child and how its mental life was organized.

Klein stressed the development of the ego as the core of the personal life. In this she side-tracked but did not abandon the topography of Freud's id and superego. The ego was the center of the developing child's world. It was the ego, as it came to stand for the person, that had an intensely private life with the people, or, to use her word, the "objects" to whom it related. For Klein, the instincts sought objects as their aim, rather than pleasure as Freud posited. The objects—the people—were, however, objects of an internal nature rather than the images of the actual people in the child's life. The internal objects were part of the heritage that an infant brought into the world along with instincts. Where an instinct arose so did an image of an object to satisfy it. Real people were screens upon which the infant could project its internal fantasies. Experience of people in the world confirmed the experience of the child's internal object relations. Klein explained the inner fantasy world in terms of the struggle between the two great instincts: libido, the life force, and aggression, the death instinct. These two instinctual forces met in the individual's psyche and formed the battleground on which the ego developed. Klein discussed how, at the beginning of life, the baby begins to take into itself the good experiences at the breast and to project from itself onto the breast the bad experiences. Thus the mother's breast, and later, when the infant can experience a whole person, the

31

mother, become both the good and the bad object. In later life, all people intimately connected with the person become a projection screen for the internal
objects of the individual's psyche.

What Klein saw in her practice was in fact much richer than her explanation claims, for her observations are continually short-circuited by her insis-
tence on inner psychic life as instinctual rather than social. For feminism, the
most profound of her discoveries lies in the early object relationships of mother-
raised children. Her shift of emphasis to early life and the construction of personality in the first few years brings into the arena (although Klein herself does
not emphasize this) the importance of the early acquisition of femininity and
masculinity, long before the Freudian oedipal phase. Another important aspect
of Klein's early object relations work is forcefully argued by Dorothy Dinnerstein in *The Mermaid and the Minotaur:* Since all infants organize their internal life around the person of the mother, and all infants have good and bad
experiences at the mother's breast and in her social arena, and since all infants
come to identify with the person of the caregiver, who is at once both the loved
one and the feared and hated one, then all children raised by women take into
themselves a picture of woman as both all-good and powerful on the one hand
and all-bad and withholding on the other. Dinnerstein, using Kleinian theory,
thus explains the misogynist nature of all our psychologies.

Ronald Fairbairn was the first analyst to depart radically from Freud's instinct theory and to revise libido theory. Fairbairn developed an object relations
theory of ego development based on social relationships. He was greatly influenced by the work of Melanie Klein, but whereas Klein maintained instincts
theory and placed much emphasis on the world of internalized objects, Fairbairn dismissed the notion of instincts as primary determinants in the formation
of the psyche, and posited a materialist view of ego development. He believed
that the significance of the object to the person was not as a means of instinctual gratification, but in terms of its essential place in the development of the ego;
that the ego, the person, the self, develops only in relationships. Whereas
Freud saw libido as primarily seeking satisfaction, Fairbairn believed that the
individual has a drive for relationship, a drive for contact with another human
being. Thus the infant has a primary need for human contact. Ego development
begins at birth and in relation to the primary caregiver, the mother. This early
period, which Fairbairn calls "infantile dependence," is the pivotal period in
ego development.

Fairbairn saw that in the course of ego development a part of the person
withdraws and goes into hiding. Fairbairn calls this "withdrawal," this split in
the ego, the "schizoid" split, and it is a major part of his work on schizoid
personalities. In discussing these personalities Fairbairn suggests that anxiety
arises out of the experience of not having needs attended to. To deal with the
anxiety, the person denies the need. In denying the need, the person is cutting
off a part of himself or herself, hiding it from the outer world and relationships.
The split ego, one part of which has now withdrawn into an inner world, experiences a sense of futility and hopelessness. The longed-for, potentially satisfying object seems farther and farther away. In adult life, schizoid people (and we

should add here that to some extent, according to Fairbairn, everyone has a schizoid split) feel themselves to have a private part of their personality which is kept hidden from others. The person may feel that the part which is in the world and seen by others is somehow inauthentic. The schizoid person often feels cut off and apart from other people. Only within intimate, safe relationships does the hidden part have the possibility of emerging.

Since W. D. Winnicott's professional interest in psychoanalysis evolved from his experience with children as a pediatrician, the insights and the far-reaching effects of his work were built upon his observations of the early relationship between infant and mother. Winnicott's emphasis was on the very early stages of life outside the womb. Although very much in the psychoanalytic tradition, his work was a decisive shift away from the formulations of Freud and Klein, for he was in essence a materialist. His famous remark, "There is no such thing as an infant, meaning, of course, that wherever one finds an infant one finds maternal care, and without maternal care there would be no infant," places the emphasis on the relationship between infant and caregiver that allows the baby to become a person. Winnicott coined the phrase ego relatedness, by which he meant the capacity of the ego to develop a sense of security within itself and its environment through what he called "good enough mothering." Focusing on the period just before and after birth, he writes of the identification mothers feel with their infants, their capacity to empathize, to provide a psychic umbilical cord that nourishes the developing ego. He also uses the terms true self and false self. The true self is the very core of human existence, the capacity to relate to oneself and others. The false self arises as a protection against an undernourished ego that feels no security. Shortcomings or failures in early maternal nurturance lead to false selves and inhibit the development of a whole ego.

Winnicott made a major contribution to the theory and practice of psychotherapy by implementing in his therapeutic work his understanding of early processes. But although Winnicott's work is extremely useful, he accepts that the pattern of childrearing in contemporary society is sound, and that the problems caused by poor mothering relate only to a fault in the particular mother-child relationship, rather than to flaws in present child-rearing arrangements.

Harry Guntrip, an analysand of Fairbairn, took up the contributions of Fairbairn and Winnicott and extended the analysis of the developmental stage of schizoid phenomena. He understood that this early dynamic of splitting was critical in the formation of aspects of the personality. His modesty and his clear exposition of Fairbairn's and Winnicott's work make it difficult to know where his particular contribution started and theirs ended. Most striking is the humanity he brought to his understanding of the person and the relationship of self and others. Guntrip's clinical work was clearly of a radical nature. He was most insistent on the quality of the therapeutic relationship and the need for the therapist to locate the unintegrated or hidden self that the schizoid personality reveals in the safety of a trusting relationship. He, along with Winnicott, saw therapy with distressed people as repair work that would restart the maturational processes that had been halted. What comes across clearly in Guntrip's

33

descriptions of his work and clients is the importance of nurturance within the therapy relationship. This concept is a cornerstone of our feminist psychotherapy.

While our theory shares much with the work of Fairbairn, Guntrip, and Winnicott, we must stress where we diverge from the object relations theorists. For we acknowledge that mother is not an object, mother is a person, a social and psychological being. From this perspective, what becomes internalized is not the object, but the different aspects of mother. What the object relations theorists have failed to take into account is the psychology of the mother and the effect of the social position of women on the mother's psychology.

14. See especially, Harry Guntrip, *Schizoid Phenomena and Object Relations Theory,* London 1968; D. W. Winnicott, *Through Pediatrics to Psychoanalysis,* London 1975; Michael Balint, *Primary Love and Psychoanalytic Technique,* London, 1952.

15. The term ego is used by different schools of psychoanalysis in different ways. We use ego to mean the emotional and psychological life of the person, including unconscious and conscious aspects of the personality. It includes the whole psychic structure, as opposed to Freud's construction of id, ego, superego.

16. See René A. Spitz, *The First Year of Life: A Psychoanalytic Study of Normal and Deviant Development of Object Relations,* New York, 1961. Spitz argues convincingly that it is early parenting that allows for the survival and growth of an infant into a human being.

17. "It could be objected that the mother is not the only human being in the child's environment, not the only one who has an emotional influence, that his environment comprises father, siblings, relatives and others, who all may have an affective significance for the child. Even the cultural setting and its mores have an influence on the child already during the first year of life. All this is self-evident; however, we do not always remember that in our Western culture these influences are transmitted to the child by the mother or her substitute . . . one might say that mother is the representative of the environment." Spitz, *The First Year of Life,* p. 101.

18. "Maturity and the capacity to be alone implies that the individual has had a chance through good enough mothering to build up a belief in a benign environment." D. W. Winnicott, *The Capacity To Be Alone in the Maturational Processes and the Facilitating Environment,* London, 1976, p. 32.

19. As Dorothy Dinnerstein has pointed out (*The Mermaid and the Minotaur: Sexual Arrangements and Human Malaise,* New York, 1976, p. 112):

So long as the first parent is a woman, then woman will inevitably be pressed in to the dual role of indispensable quasi-human supporter and deadly quasi-human enemy of the human self. She will be seen as naturally fit to nurture other people's individuality; as the born audience in whose awareness other people's subjective existence can be mirrored; as the being so peculiarly needed to confirm other people's worth, power, significance, that if she fails to render them this service she is a monster, anomalous and useless. And at the same time she will also be seen as the one who will not let other people be, the one who beckons her loved ones from selfhood, who wants to engulf, dissolve, drown, suffocate them as autonomous persons.

20. M. S. Mahler, et al., *The Psychological Birth of the Human Infant: Symbiosis and Individuation,* New York and London, 1975. Margaret Mahler and her colleagues observed many infant-caregiver interactions and drew a picture of the transition from infant to toddler, stressing the development of psychic structuralization. Mahler saw that the baby becomes human within human relationships, that the psychological birth of the human infant is a process that occurs outside the womb and is shaped in relationships.

21. On this point we are in some disagreement with Robert Stoller and Nancy Chodorow, who focus on the difficulties boys have in separation because of their original merger with mother. They believe boys' separation difficulties are compounded by this gender difference, whereas we believe their gender difference aids them in separation.

22. R. J. Stoller, *Sex and Gender,* New York, 1968, London, 1969.

23. The anthropological studies of Margaret Mead show the plasticity of these variations in cross-cultural settings. She observed that "in all cultures, without any exception, male activity is seen as achievement; whatever women do—gathering seeds, planting, weeding, basket-making, pot-making—is valued less than when the same activity in some other culture is performed by men." (Jean Strouse, ed., *Women and Analysis*). Further, Mead discovered that a quality may be assigned to females in one culture and in another praised as a male attribute: "Now it is boys who are thought of as infinitely vulnerable and in need of special cherishing care, now it is girls. In some societies it is girls for whom parents must collect a dowry or make husband-catching magic, in others the parents' worry is over the difficulty of marrying off the boys" (*Male and Female,* Harmondsworth, 1976, p. 30).

24. J. Money and A. Erhardt, *Man and Woman, Boy and Girl: The Differentiation and Dimorphism of Gender Identity from Conception to Maturity,* Baltimore, Md., 1972, London, 1973.

CHAPTER 2

The Construction of Femininity

The girl, because of her deep emotional tie with her mother and her recognition of her as being the same, is driven to choose her as a model and to reproduce this model faithfully in herself. The mother's behavior, her reactions, the relationship between the girl and the mother, and between the mother and every other member of the family, all indicate the values to which the mother herself responds (through the unconscious process of identification). The essence of the mother penetrates the girl and is absorbed by her. This means that everything depends on what the mother is like. But however exceptional she may be, she remains a woman; a being with lower social value than the man's, for whom tasks of secondary importance are reserved. If this is the model the girl must interiorize, girls have little reason to rejoice.

ELENA GIANNINI BELOTTI
Little Girls

PSYCHOLOGICAL development starts at birth and occurs within the context of the relationship the infant has with the caregiver. Women's psychological development is thus shaped in the mother-daughter relationship, the critical relationship in the formation of women's psychology.

Mothers and daughters share a gender identity, a social role, and social expectations. They are both second-class citizens within a patriarchal culture and the family. In mothering a baby girl a woman is bringing her daughter up to be like her, to be a girl and then a woman. In mothering her son she is bringing him up to be other, to be a boy and then a man. Because of the social consequences of gender, mothers inevitably relate differently to their daughters and their sons. Much of the difference is intentional and prescribed by the requirements of sex-role stereotyping—for example, encouraging an adolescent son's sexual adventures and restricting an adolescent daughter's. Some of the difference is subtle and mothers may not be aware of it—girls are encouraged to be neat, messiness is tolerated in boys; or girls are encouraged to be "pretty" and boys to be "bright." And some of the difference comes from a mother's unconscious feelings about being a woman and raising a daughter or raising a son.

In looking at the significance of the shared gender of mothers and daughters, the most obvious and most important point is that all mothers were and are daughters themselves. A second obvious and important point is that all daughters are brought up by their mothers to become mothers. The third point is that all mothers learned from their mothers about their place in the world. In each woman's experience is the memory, buried or active, of the struggles she had with her mother in the process of becoming a woman, of learning to curb her activities and to direct her interests in particular ways. Mothers and daughters thus have a tremendous amount of common experience, although this is often obscured by the fact that they are always in different phases of their social role vis-à-vis each other. A fifty-year-old mother and a twenty-five-year-old mother each experiences similar emotional pushes and pulls in relation to their children. Yet the mothering requirements for each of them are very different. Adult women with girl children play two roles simultaneously in the mother-daughter relationship: they are their mother's daughters and their daughter's mothers.

The interplay between a woman's conscious and unconscious feelings about being both a daughter and a mother are an essential part of what she brings to maternal nurturance. The psychology that the infant girl will embody in the process of becoming a person will be imbued with the mother's sense of self. Growing up female and being a woman means that one's sense of self reflects what each woman has had to learn in her development. Aspects of the mother's psychology that are inextricably bound up with being socialized to the feminine role are absorbed and then shared by the daughter in her own psychology.

In our practice we often hear women describe how startling it is to hear themselves speaking to their daughters just as their mothers spoke to them. As one woman put it, "I couldn't believe it came out of my mouth. The same tone of voice, practically the very same words. It was as if my mother's voice came from my lips." It is often after a woman has a child that she becomes more aware of the ways in which she is like her mother. The mother's influence becomes apparent as aspects of her personality resonate for the daughter in herself as mother. Traversing the generations from grandmother to mother to daughter is a particular psychology which has its roots and its flesh in the experience of being female in a patriarchal culture. The social requirements of deference, submission, and passivity generate many complicated feelings. Often women do not feel complete, substantial, or good within themselves. They feel afraid of their emotional needs, their insecurities and dependencies; they are fearful and guilty about their sexuality and their strivings for independence, nurturance, and power. The social requirements of patriarchy surround a girl from the moment of her birth. This means that she has a particular psychology which she transmits to her daughter.

Men's and women's psychologies reflect patriarchal attitudes in different ways. A boy will be raised to expect to be looked after and attended to, a girl to provide the looking after and attending.

For a woman, the process of pregnancy, giving birth, and becoming a mother can be a very satisfying experience. Having a baby may fulfill an important personal desire and enrich a woman's sense of self. Since motherhood is traditionally the apex of woman's social role, approved by family and society, giving birth enables a woman to feel a certain contentment. In turn she is able to transmit these positive feelings to her daughter. Mother reads the communications of her daughter and is responsive. The infant in turn expresses her pleasure, and this communication adds to mother's feelings of self-worth and potency. Positive interactions between mother and daughter establish a pattern of relating and a feeling of closeness between them. As a relationship forms, the mother experiences great pleasure in seeing her daughter's daily developments. Mother's time and care and tiring long hours of work through the day and night have moments of overpowering reward as she sees her daughter grow, and she continues to express her feelings of competence, strength, and ability to care and protect within the relationship. In this nurturing relationship the mother gives her daughter the essential emotional food that helps the infant establish her very sense of existence as well as her security and well-being. The daughter's psychological development is built on the feelings of acceptance and love in this first and most important relationship.

Beyond these positive feelings that mother has toward

herself, however, lie mother's other experiences of self. The effect of having to curtail one's wants and desires over many years is that many women are not aware of the fact that they feel needy, and they have complicated feelings about their repressed needs. Over the years in our practice we have seen many women reveal the part of them that is needy and uncared for, undeserving, inadequate, and inarticulate. A woman often feels that nobody sees this part of her or gives her what she needs, and that even she herself cannot locate what she wants—"everybody sees me as so strong, they don't know that I have my moments, too, when I want to give up and weep and feel unsure and anxious." These negative and complicated feelings, conscious or unconscious, also have a profound effect on the daughter's psychology. The mother's negative self-image is as important a factor in the mother-daughter interaction, and hence in the daughter's psychology, as her positive experiences of self through motherhood and in other areas.

We can identify the following major aspects of the mother-daughter interaction which make for a particular shaping of a daughter's psychology. The first of these is that the mother will *identify* with her daughter because of their shared gender, for when a woman gives birth to a daughter she is in a sense reproducing herself. When she looks at her daughter she sees herself. Laura, a thirty-three-year-old mother of a daughter aged three and (an infant) son, talked about this point in her therapy. "When Ruth was an infant I can remember looking down at my body as I lay in a certain position in my bed and thinking it was Ruth's body. The shape of my knee or my arm looked to me like Ruth's body. And when she had her first cold I felt ill. It was very strange. These things have not happened with Barry. Somehow it just isn't the same. I've never had the feeling I *was* him or he *was* me."

Vivian, a forty-year-old woman, expressed it this way: "When my daughter was born, each time I looked at her I thought she *was* me; I couldn't tell at all that she was different from me. You know that feeling when you look at yourself in a mirror? Well, it felt something like that. When my son was born that never even crossed my mind. He was different, he was something else [motioning "out there" and "away" with her hand]. It was completely clear that he was a different person."

When a mother looks at an infant son she sees someone who is quite other, who is going to have a very different life, and for whom she can imagine a whole world of differing possibilities. But she knows that her daughter will follow her own footsteps. Mother must introduce her daughter to the ways of behaving and feeling that go along with being a girl. Mother must prepare her for a life spent, like hers, in taking care of others. Mother, whether she is consciously aware of it or not, must also prepare her daughter to take her place in society as a second-class citizen.

When a woman bears a son, the difference in sex and gender helps her to be more aware of her own boundaries. A woman does not have this aid with a daughter. The boundaries are blurred. When she looks at her daughter she sees mirror images of her own experience of being mothered, her own childhood and growing up; her whole life as a woman.

The second major aspect of the mother-daughter relationship is that a mother not only identifies with her daughter but also *projects* onto her some of the feelings she has about herself. Having superimposed these deeply buried feelings which are inaccessible and unconscious she experiences them as if expressed in her daughter. In this projection she is seeing her daughter not as another person but as an extension of herself. Thus when she holds her infant daughter in her arms she reads the child's communications in a particular way. She sees a vulnerable, undefended, expressive, eager little girl. This in turn reawakens—still at an unconscious level—the part of her that feels needy and wants to be nurtured, responded to, encouraged.

Such feelings are almost inevitable because of the importance in women's social role, and thus in their psychology, of deferring to and caring for others. Women today pay a high psychological price for the ability to nurture. In developing emotional antennae for the desires of others, women place their own needs second. The experience of receiving nurturance is not symmetrical for women and men. There is an unequal emotional exchange between men and women, and the emotional caretaking is not reciprocal. Because of this social-psychological construct a woman hides and represses many of her own emotional needs as she develops an adult stance in the world. She appears to be a person with little need. These needs do not disappear, however, and in experiencing and responding to the needs of her infant daughter the mother unconsciously first identifies and then projects her *own* needy parts, what we call her little-girl onto her daughter.

In responding to her daughter the mother is full of contradictory feelings, some conscious and some not. She wants to meet her daughter's needs: sometimes she is able to and at other times she is not. The reasons are complex. On the one hand she hopes for a fuller and less restricted life for her daughter, while on the other she is fearful for a daughter who does not learn the essential feminine characteristics of restraining her own needs and desires and curbing her moves toward independence. This conflict is often unconscious. Mothers generally raise and relate to their daughters much as they themselves were raised. Unbeknownst to them they are caught in a paradox. Mother has the difficult task of showing her daughter how to limit her strivings toward independence. At the same time she must wean her very early from relying, at an emotional level, upon having her dependency desires met. For mother to continue to meet them would go deeply against the grain of socialization to the feminine role. Mother knows that she has had to manage and contain her own desires for emotional nurturance; that she has had to swallow her disappointment and anger many times and that she has had to learn how to adjust her expectations for emotional care and relating.

Their own social experience prevents mothers from setting up false expectations about what awaits a daughter in womanhood. Unconsciously mother gives the message to the daughter: "Don't be emotionally dependent; don't expect the emotional care and attention you want; learn to stand on your own two feet emotionally. Don't expect too much independence; don't expect too much from a man; don't be too wild; don't expect a life much different from mine; learn to accommodate." Mother demonstrates these unconscious injunctions by relating to her daughter in this way herself. Consciously and unconsciously mother acts toward her daughter in the ways she experiences others relating to herself. Unable to respond continually and directly to her daughter's needs because her own needs have not been met in this way, she relates to the child inconsistently.

At times the mother is able to see her daughter as a separate little person and to respond to her freely. At other times, however, the mother's unconscious identification makes her annoyed with the child for displaying her needs and for not controlling them as she herself does. At these times mother is unconsciously driven to respond to her daughter with resentment and disapproval, thus transmitting the message that there is something wrong with her daughter, something wrong with her desires, something that needs to be kept at bay. Unwittingly, mother provides her daughter with her first lesson in emotional deprivation.

At the same time that mother pushes her daughter's neediness away she pulls her daughter to stay within the boundaries that she herself inhabits. There is a push-pull dynamic in the mother-daughter relationship. Mother wishes to see her daughter contented, but she is again caught in a paradox, for she herself does not have the experience of contentment. Mother has learned throughout her childhood to curb her desires and wants, to split her needs off, to hide that part of herself from others and not to expect to be responded to. Mother herself has a little-girl hidden inside herself.

This repressed little-girl inside mother is a third important shaper of the mother-daughter relationship. Mother comes to be frightened by her daughter's free expression of her needs, and unconsciously acts toward her infant daughter in the same way she acts internally toward the little-girl part of herself. In some ways the little daughter becomes an external representation of that part of herself which she has come to dislike and deny. The complex of emotions that results from her own deprivation through childhood and adult life is both directed inward in the struggle to negate the little-girl part of herself and projected outward onto her daughter.

A vivid example of this dynamic is the relationship between Beth and her daughter Alice. Beth is a forty-three-year-old mother of two children; Paul is twenty and Alice eighteen. Beth and Alice's relationship is an extremely rocky one. They quarrel frequently and there are many dramatic scenes in the household. Beth feels that she has never had an easy time with Alice. Beth describes her experience with Paul as pleasurable and fulfilling. He was a "good baby" who gave her few problems. Beth says, "From the time Alice was an infant she was always difficult. Nothing I ever did satisfied her. She cried all the time and made me feel totally inadequate. As a little girl she was angry with me a lot, and at the same time she was very clingy. She used to have nightmares regularly and would come into my bed at night. She always seemed so greedy. Whatever I gave her was never enough. Now that she's a teenager she's just impossible. She has awful friends who just hang around on street corners. She's nearly gotten expelled from school twice. When she got pregnant I thought I couldn't take any more. I just don't know what to do with her." At other times in her therapy Beth described the ways that Alice upset her as her son and her husband never did. She felt guilty in relation to Alice, and this underlying guilt always forced her to "give in" and "pick up the pieces after her." Beth described her daughter as a "wicked little girl," a powerful person with the ability to be highly destructive.

Beth presents herself as a very capable woman. She was divorced when the children were eight and ten, and went back to work as a librarian. She supports the family, takes adult education courses, to "improve" herself, and is involved in community politics. Beth has hidden her own needs so successfully that when asked in therapy when and by whom she gets care and love she could barely understand the question.

To illustrate the complex psychological merger between Alice and Beth, we first need to describe a bit about Beth's relationship to her own mother, a housewife who had three children. From very early in her life Beth can remember her attempts at separating from her "controlling" mother. She had to define herself in opposition to her mother in order to keep her from invading all of Beth's experiences. From childhood Beth acted as if she could stand on her own two feet and resisted all her mother's attempts to help her. At the same time she had to hide all her needs. She unconsciously felt she could not afford to expose them, for if she did mother would take over. To preserve herself Beth repressed her needs, her upsets, her vulnerabilities—the little-girl inside. As a teenager she did well at school and seemed happy in her excellence. Her friends saw Beth as a competent, forceful woman in the world, a woman who could go through a difficult marriage and divorce and come out of it seemingly stronger. Her friends thought her "a remarkable woman."

When Beth gave birth to Alice something in her was touched that had not been touched when Paul was born. Giving birth to a girl caused a psychological eruption. Up to that point she had managed her own yearnings and needs and kept them in check, but her unconscious identification with her infant daughter aroused her own dependency feelings, her yearnings and internal cries for care, love, and attention. Because her protective defenses were shaken, her daughter seemed a powerful and destructive person. In the first months of Alice's life, Beth struggled to regain her equilibrium, to recapture the feeling of competence she had experienced with Paul. But she could not. Every cry and communication of need that Alice transmitted upset her.

In her struggle for psychological equilibrium, Beth tried desperately to deny and negate her own feelings as they surfaced. At the same time she was unintentionally rejecting Alice. Her unspoken communications to Alice shouted to the baby not to need or want, to shut up and be satisfied. A grueling cycle began as the baby felt her mother's tension, anger, and rejection, and became more and more upset herself. As the child grew older she too curbed her neediness and developed her own little-girl inside, so that her psychological split in many ways mirrored her mother's. However, Alice was angry and rebellious about her deprivation and restriction. Unable to let go of her anger and her need, she fought her mother continually and showed them in altered forms such as the pregnancy and the troubles at school.

In Beth's therapy we were able to see the ways in which her daughter expressed many of Beth's own feelings and desires. Gradually Beth was able to see her identification with Alice and to see the ways she had rejected the child just as she rejected the little-girl part of herself.

This mother-daughter relationship illustrates the sensitivity that a mother can develop toward the needs and desires of a daughter, needs and desires that imitate her own. These features of mother-daughter interaction make for extreme intensity in the relationship. This intensity is often marked by a staccato quality, an inconsistency in the relating. The inconsistency stems from the way a mother copes with her feeling of identification with her daughter and her own deep feelings about herself as a woman. At those times when mother relates to daughter as a separate person she can be responsive and unambiguously caring. She can give her daughter what she needs and convey a sense of security and well-being. At other times, however, mother's sense of herself as a separate person dissolves and she experiences her daughter and herself as having the same feelings, thoughts, and desires.[1] When this occurs it is hard for a mother to be appropriately responsive; she may be withdrawn at one moment and overinvolved the next. She is acting on her unconscious feelings of identification and relating to her daughter in the same inconsistent way that she relates to the little-girl part of herself. Such toing and froing between a mother's sense of herself as separate and her merger with her daughter creates the staccato quality in the relationship.

The shape of this relationship, first established in infancy, is maintained throughout the daughter's life. As she slowly becomes her own person and needs her mother in different ways, the intense push-pull nature of the relationship persists. The daughter is absorbing essential lessons about what it means to be female, with her mother as both model and guide, and beyond that their relationship is absorbed by the daughter as a blueprint for other love relationships. The picture of mother that the daughter takes into herself is complex. Mother is the person who gives her what she needs—feeds her, bathes her, cuddles her, plays with her, talks to her, responds to her. She opens up wider and wider horizons. At the same time mother is the person who can say no, who can disappoint or withhold, who can be short-tempered and can misunderstand. Mother holds tremendous power to please and to hurt.

Many of mother's actions are thus incomprehensible, because the daughter receives contradictory messages in the push-pull dynamic. She experiences her mother giving the unconscious injunctions of staying close by but not expecting too much for doing so. The little girl cannot fathom why mother is so approving and loving at times and so disappointed and disappointing at others. The little girl tries to make sense of mother's actions. The part of her that has felt nurtured and understood by mother has contributed to a psychological experience of solidity and goodness, but she has also experienced that some parts of herself are not acceptable. The little girl absorbs the idea that to get love and approval she must show a particular side of herself. She must hide her emotional cravings, her disappointments and her angers, her fighting spirit. She must hide *her self.* She comes to feel that there must be something wrong with who she really is, which in turn must mean there is something wrong with what she needs and what she wants. A feeling that she is inauthentic develops, and she is unsure in her reactions and distanced from her wants. This soon translates into feeling unworthy and hesitant about pursuing her impulses. Slowly she develops an acceptable self, one that appears self-sufficient and capable and will receive more consistent acceptance. Here in this first relationship with mother the little girl learns to fear and hide away the little-girl part of herself. And she comes to feel like a fraud, for an external part of her is developing that is different from who she feels she is inside.

Here we can begin to see the way in which a feminine psychology is reproduced from generation to generation. Girls' psychologies develop within the context of their social world and social role. In our practice we hear women talk about their needs with contempt, humiliation, and shame. They feel exposed and childish, greedy and insatiable. Mothers and daughters both attempt to curb their little-girl inside while showing only one part of themselves to others, a part they feel others will find acceptable because it is not needy.

This psychological split, which occurs in the first years of life, is not a conscious act but a protective feature of psychic structural development. The hidden part (the little-girl) does not disappear; it has to go underground and seek nurturance within the girl's inner world. And since this little-girl part of the developing psyche still yearns for nurturance, there is confusion about its rejection in the first place. This part of the psyche tends to carry feelings of isolation and depression, even despair. When contact with it is evoked she may be flooded with feelings of anger, disappointment, or rejection. Hurt by the mother's rejections, the daughter may not be able to show this needy part to anyone again, and so lives primarily in her inner world of relationships (internal object relations). These both excite and disappoint her little-girl inside. As we saw in chapter 1 the girl constructs seemingly more satisfactory relationships in her inner world. Mother continues to live on inside, alternately presenting herself as giver and withholder. She is still very powerful and still much needed. Inside too, the little-girl is trying to challenge the deep conviction that if she shows herself she will continue to be rejected and disliked. In her private world the child tries to rewrite history, but time and again her previous painful experiences are reinforced. So the little-girl part builds boundaries; it is as though the needy, frightened part is surrounded by a fortress. She cannot send messages out and others cannot penetrate her defenses. Nobody can come in and hurt her and she cannot get out and hurt others or humiliate herself by exposing her needs.

Giselle is a thirty-six-year-old woman with a son of nine. Since the age of twenty-two Giselle has been in psychiatric hospitals three times, each time because her emotional distress was so great that she appeared to be unable to function in her daily activities. In the course of Giselle's therapy we came to understand why at those times in her life when she felt great pressure and emotional upset, she withdrew into herself completely. She could not manage her feelings and felt that no one was there to help her with them. Giselle was an only child. Her father left when Giselle was six months old, and her mother worked to support the two of them and at the same time managed to have a social life of her own, going out with men on occasion. Giselle's experience was that from very early in her life she had to cope quietly with her feelings. She clung to her mother as her sole parent, and was terrified when her mother was angry or annoyed with her. She was praised for being a pretty little girl and a good little girl, not a needy little girl. It was almost as if she and her mother were friends and roommates rather than mother and dependent daughter. Giselle's little-girl inside became so barricaded behind protective defenses that she rarely emerged in any form.

Several years into her therapy Giselle had a dream in which she was on a small island waving from a window of a brick, castlelike building. This dream represented a turning point in the therapy; Giselle's little-girl was obviously pleading to be seen and saved. After the dream, Giselle's therapy proceeded, and she was able to see that her mother had struggled to support her daughter economically but could not provide an adequate emotional support system.

This is often the case even in families with economic stability. A daughter hides the little-girl part of herself because she has picked up a painful and powerful message from mother that tells her she should not have expectations of being looked after emotionally, or of having her desires met, either by mother or by anyone else. Mother encourages her daughter to look to a man to be emotionally involved with; she teaches her daughter to direct her energies toward men and to someday depend on a man. But at the same time there is another message. As she lets her daughter know she must look to men, mother simultaneously transmits a message of disappointment and frustration. She conveys that her daughter must not expect a man to really help or understand her. Mothers often let their daughters know both overtly and covertly that men are disappointments. They may convey disdain and contempt for them. Mother's messages about men are thus more than a little ambivalent. She conveys both the necessity and the limitations of a daughter's emotional ties to a man.

Lorraine was perplexed by her mother's interest in the job

status of the men she went out with. Her mother seemed terribly interested in these relationships, yet Lorraine always felt uncomfortable about discussing them with her mother because she realized that her mother had very little interest in what Lorraine felt about the personalities of her men friends. Indeed, her mother never discussed men in terms of emotional exchange or feelings. On a conscious level Lorraine felt pressure from her mother to find the right man and settle down, but on another level she felt that her mother dismissed men completely, that she didn't think of them as people capable of relationships or feelings. Consciously the mother was pushing her daughter to be with a man, but unconsciously, she was transmitting a message not to expect anything from a man except a house and children. Lorraine began to understand that essentially her mother thought of men as economic providers and that was all.

Even though a daughter comes to look toward men, she still yearns for mother's support and care. From girlhood to womanhood women live with the experience of having lost these aspects of maternal nurturance. This nurturance is never replaced. Women look to men to mother them but remain bereft. These needs for nurturance do not decrease any the less for loss. This loss, which causes tremendous pain, confusion, disappointment, rage, and guilt for the daughter, is buried and denied in the culture at large as well as in the unconscious of the little girl.

We have mentioned that infants who have had sufficient good contact to embody the caregiver's positive feelings within themselves come to feel secure. They are confident that their needs will be met and that the large world they can now see outside themselves and mother is full of exciting possibilities and new relationships. As the baby begins to separate from mother she or he acquires a sense of individuality. For the developing girl, still yearning for mother's reassurance, psychological separation and individuation can only be partial. The experience of the initial relating with mother means that the girl is left with feelings of deprivation, unworthiness, and rejection. As she still needs mother very badly it is hard for her to feel unambiguously receptive to new experiences or to have confidence that others will be receptive to her needs and desires. She tries to move toward others to express herself but she feels nervous, at once disloyal and abandoned. Enjoying being with an aunt may be complicated; she may seek contact with her and yet feel guilty for leaving mother and for getting nurturance from elsewhere. This is an example of the way in which the social requirement for women to be connected to others rather than full, autonomous people is reflected in the development of a feminine psychology.

Too often a little girl's attempts at separation take place under conditions of opposition from mother and consequent fear. There is no feeling of strength and wholeness to make the world outside seem exciting; instead it is tantalizing and frightening. In some ways it echoes aspects of the painful inner world of the child's reality. Mother is still a focal point; she encourages some attempts at separation—even forces them—and thwarts others. Because the little-girl part of the girl's psyche has been split off, it continues to be deprived of the nourishment and contact it needs for maturation. The girl both fears and longs to remerge with mother and to be held and cared for, but the inconsistencies in the relationship push her toward separation, with the construction of boundaries between self and the little-girl inside. These are in some sense false boundaries; they do not come from an integrated ego structure which can clearly distinguish between self and the outside world, but are internal boundaries, separating one part of herself from another part and keeping the little-girl inside shut away from the outside world.

At the same time, the daughter's sense of self is fused with her sense of mother, so that in her attempts to separate from mother she may not know who she herself is. Trying to be her own person, she is nevertheless confused about where she begins and mother ends. In her early development she has taken mother into her, and now, because she does not have a strong sense of her own separate self, the sense of mother inside her may outweigh her own independent identity. Unlike her brother, she cannot use gender difference to differentiate herself. Psychologically and socially she is a miniversion of mother, someone who will have a life like mother's.

And so her sense of self as unique, separate, and other is entwined with a sense of mother. There is a shared social role, a shared prescription for life, and a shared psychology.

Inevitably, then, the daughter's attempts at separation are somewhat ambiguous and dovetail with mother's ambivalence. The message from mother during the period of infantile dependency has been, "Take care of yourself, don't depend on others, don't want too much," but these injunctions, which in effect seem to push the daughter away, have been combined with the unstated, unconscious message: "Stay close, don't stray, don't go too far, it's dangerous." As a result, the process toward separation has to contend with a tug to stay close to mother and share the boundaries she inhabits.

Ideally, as daughter tries to separate from mother, mother in turn must let go just enough. She must allow her daughter to explore the limits of her developing identity from a secure base. The broadening of boundaries and setting of new ones that daughter and mother negotiate require enormous emotional and psychological shifting for the mother. In the daughter's infancy the mother may experience a tension between her sense of the baby's utter dependency and helplessness, which confirms her essentiality, and her desires for the child's separateness. The mother may be reassured by being needed and simultaneously resent and begrudge her own loss of independence. If she worked outside the home before the birth and intends to do so again, she must shift her focus from her former job to that of child rearing and then remove herself psychologically and emotionally from her absorption in her infant's world back toward the outside world and her other work.[2]

There is a delicate pushing away and pulling together between mother and baby as each attempts to separate from the other. Mother's wish to keep her daughter close reflects her own psychology and social experience. Having a child has filled up her life, and if she has been living through her child, accruing an identity through mothering, she may have great difficulty letting her daughter separate. She may need to keep her daughter close to her to maintain this sense of herself, and this psychological need may exist whether or not she has worked outside the home. A daughter's moves toward independence are bound to diminish a mother's sense of being needed. Brought up to see her central role as that of mother, she may feel empty, depressed, confused about who she is; she may lose her sense of purpose. If she has not been able to separate psychologically from her mother, she may in turn cling to her daughter. The period of her child's separation-individuation can make the mother feel that she is already "losing" her child, in a foretaste of future separations (nursery school, adolescence) that jolts and hurts. She clings in the hope that her daughter will not abandon her.

If the mother's psychological development has been similar to her daughter's, and she herself has not had a solid experience of separation and selfhood, she too has false boundaries. Her daughter's moving away involves a loss at the psychic structural level because she has attempted to complete herself in her attachment to and merger with her daughter. The distinction between the two of them is blurred, so that the daughter's development toward independence brings feelings of loss as well as pride.

As a baby daughter reaches this stage, a woman often finds herself wanting another baby. "I thought I wanted only one child," said one of our clients. "I never intended to have more. But when Jennie was two I started having dreams about another baby and thinking about it every single day. I sort of forgot about my previous thoughts on the subject of how many children I wanted. It wasn't on a rational, thinking level. I just *felt* intensely that I wanted another baby." Mother's unconscious feelings of loss as her daughter attempts separation constantly reinforce the jagged attachment between the two of them. As mother now pulls her daughter to stay close, as she indicates to her the shape of a girl's life, she instructs her in an essential feminine skill. She teaches her to look after others. The daughter, as she learns to hide her needy little-girl part, becomes extremely sensitive to neediness in others. She develops the radar to pick up the needs of others; *she learns to give what others need; and she gives to others out of the well of her own unmet needs.*

Once again we see the reproduction of a feminine psychology. Just as mother responds to and anticipates the needs of others, and just as mother identifies with the yearnings and needs of others, so the daughter comes to embody this same capacity for giving. And like mother, she too wishes for someone to respond to her needs. So the giving capaci-

The Construction of Femininity

ty starts very early on in her life and becomes an important part of her identity and self-image.

As the mother transmits to her daughter the importance of caring for others, she brings to the relationship her *own* unmet emotional needs. Inside each mother lives a hungry, needy, deprived, and angry little-girl. She turns to her daughter for nurturance, looking to the child to make up the loss of her own maternal nurturance and satisfy her continued yearnings.

The psychological attachment and lack of separation between mothers and daughters and daughters and mothers continues through generations of women. The daughter becomes involved in a cycle that is part of each woman's experience: attempting to care for mother. As the daughter learns her role as nurturer, *her first child is her mother.*

Women do not usually bring these same needs to their sons. Built into a mother's experience with a son from the beginning of his life is the knowledge that he will become his own person in the world. She accepts the fact that he will become a man and move out into the world to create and commit himself to a family of his own. But although she expects her daughter to have a family too, she expects this to be an extension of her own family rather than a separate entity. Whether or not a woman still lives with her husband after her children are grown, her daughter tends to remain available and responsible for her care and companionship. In fact, we often see daughters-in-law taking on this responsibility as well. Although an adult daughter may resent this responsibility, at the same time she is consciously and unconsciously aware of her mother's needs. The social position of women, which often forces them to hide their loneliness or pain even from themselves, is a strong adhesive in the mother-daughter relationship.

57

Just as she transmits messages to her daughter about her role as a woman, a mother also transmits what her sexuality may be. The mother's feelings about her own body and her sexuality are a critical influence on the way a daughter will come to feel about herself. Nancy Friday writes: "When we were learning to walk, mother helped us to practice and her confidence in our success encouraged us to keep trying. When it came to sex her emotions became communicated to us too, this time what we learned from her was anxiety and failure."[3]

Our complex cultural attitudes toward women's bodies— that they are sexual, ugly, mysterious, extraordinary, dark, bloody, and bad smelling—find a place in each woman's sense of self. The female body is both degraded and deified; it is felt to be so powerful that men will destroy themselves or die for it. Female sexuality is held responsible for male sexuality and male aggression (an extreme example is the myth that it is a woman's fault if a man rapes her). Women, then, often come to their relationship with their daughters with, at the very least, apprehension about the female body and the power of female sexuality.

In the generational transmission of feminine sexuality it is mothers who begin the process of shaping a daughter's sexuality. But mother's sexuality has developed within particular constraints, so that many mothers feel uncomfortable within their own bodies and hide their sexual desires and needs. In our therapeutic work we rarely hear a woman say that sexuality was openly accepted, that the parents' sexuality was visible, that mother or father informed the girl of the changes her body would go through in a positive and exciting way, telling her that when her body became a woman's body it would be a proud, joyful transition. We hear instead remembrances of shame, embarrassment, fear; of women not liking their breasts because they are too big or too small, not liking their pubic hair, big hips, or rounded bottoms. Women also recall adolescent warnings and restrictions (boys are encouraged to be experienced). Female sexuality seems to be dangerous; it is unknown, unspoken. You must have it to become a grown-up woman and yet you must hide it. Thus many adolescent girls and young women learn to be frightened of their own sexuality and to dislike their own bodies.

At the same time many daughters perceive their mothers as nonsexual and know that they do not want to be like mother in that respect. From quite an early age they may be aware of wanting to be quite a different sort of woman. A girl may want to be "sexy," like a movie star or the woman at the beauty shop. She may feel ashamed of the way her mother dresses or embarrassed by her behavior. Whether mother conveys her sexuality through dress or physicality or hides it, it will make an impression on her daughter. The daughter compares herself to her mother as she tries to find her own independent sexuality.

As the girl's sexuality explodes during adolescence, it drives her to seek freedom and independence from her family. Her new sexual body means that she comes face to face with both her reproductive and her erotic capacities. This is a painful time for many young women, because they are already uncomfortable with their sexuality and know that women's social heritage does not allow them to act on these new desires for freedom.

The thread of sexuality is entwined in the issues of separation and merger, although its meaning is not always confluent. Sexual connection with another is in part a demonstration of a woman's attempt to separate from mother. Her physical attachment to another symbolizes her relatedness outside the family, but this new relatedness highlights the complexities of separation and attachment. In many parts of society cultural law still dictates that the only way a woman can leave her family is by starting another family. Even if she lives apart from her parents, she leaves their home only to go into her husband's. In patriarchy the daughter is passed from father to husband, as ritualized in the wedding ceremony, when the bride is "given away" by the father. But often mother is crying nearby, filled with a sense of loss due to her daughter's new attachment. The paradox lies in the fruition of mother's ambiguous message. On the one hand, mother has instructed her daughter to go toward a man; on the other, when the daughter does so it brings mother tremendous pain, for she experiences the loss of her daughter. (Mother's own memory of leaving her mother may also be unconsciously re-evoked.) The marriage highlights the cultural prohibition against separation—psychological or social—for a woman. She must leave home and yet she cannot. Women are at psychic crossroads.

A daughter's personality takes shape in her relationship with her mother, a relationship weighted heavy with longing, identification, disappointment, betrayal, anger, and guilt. As mothers transmit the knowledge of how to survive within the structure that they and all women inhabit, they bind their daughters with the chains of femininity. Thus mothers and daughters share complex and powerful emotions of love, neediness, insecurity, low self-esteem, and identification. Many women never feel free of their mothers. They are not separate people, but experience mother as living inside, judging, binding, tempting, and disappointing. At the same time mothers and daughters often feel the pain of not being able to share honestly, to show themselves to each other in direct ways.

As Adrienne Rich writes, "Mother stands for the victim in ourselves, the unfree woman, the martyr. Our personalities seem dangerously to blur and overlap with our mothers." The consequence of this painful identification is that we deny that our mother has anything to do with us: "We develop matraphobia and try to split ourselves off from her, to purge ourselves of her bondage, in a desperate attempt to know where mother ends and daughter begins, we perform radical surgery."[4]

Although the nuances and particulars of each woman's experience vary, although what each woman brings to mothering is different, and although the specifics of each mother-daughter relationship are unique, these two crucial determinants—a mother's feelings about herself and her identification with her daughter—are reproduced in all mother-daughter relationships. They are the key features in the development of a woman's psychology.

As a girl develops, her father's presence in her life continues to be very different from mother's. In a traditional family the little girl learns that father is very important to family survival, and that his daily abandonment is for the purpose of providing security, especially economic security, for the family. She learns that she must rely on him in particular ways. She also sees the complexity of mother's relationship with father. She sees how mother defers to and depends on father and she also sees that father depends on mother for many things. His daily life is an expression of his need for a woman in order to survive. His dependency needs are met in an unstated way at home, emotionally and physically.

The girl may feel excluded and pushed away from mother when father is around. She senses that she does not have the power to hold mother in the same way he does. She may feel jealous of mother's availability to another, and she may feel excluded from her parents' relationship. In her infancy she and mother were a couple; as she develops, her awareness of the world shifts and she is confronted by mother and father as a couple. She takes in how important a man, a partner, is in a woman's life. Whether the marriage is satisfactory and cooperative or not, the little girl sees the intensity of her parents' relationship, and the seeds for her own future relating to a man are fertilized. As she watches mother she learns to relate to father in specific ways. For example, most little girls learn that an important part of the relationship with father is pleasing him. They are encouraged to transfer their primary dependency from mother to father, the embodiment of all future males. This is part of learning to become a woman in a heterosexual society, and, because mother is aware of this, and how she must help her daughter to make this transfer of love and dependency needs from her to father, there is a tension expressed in the mother-daughter relationship. It shows up in the push-pull dynamic.

Both parents encourage their daughter to look to father in several ways. He is the link to the world outside the family and the daughter must use him as access to that world. Because he is more secure and sure of himself in the world, she can imagine that he will protect her. However, she cannot fully identify with father because of his sexual identity. Father encourages his daughter to charm him and a male audience, to attract and hold his attention in specifically defined feminine ways, as she will later need to do. She learns that she must not attempt to make decisions which challenge his authority; she must not show too much independence and power.

Very few little girls have much contact with their fathers in the very early period of psychological development. Father plays a tremendously important role very soon, but he builds on the ego development that has occurred between mother and daughter. Father is a person with whom the daughter can identify when she is in the process of separation-individuation, and as she tries to differentiate herself from her mother, she may try to emulate him, incorporating characteristics she admires.[5] If he is outgoing, humorous, or a good storyteller, for example, the daughter may develop these aspects in her own personality.

The father's relationship with his daughter is complex. He stands outside the physical experiences of pregnancy, birth, and lactation. He may feel excluded from the mother-child relationship or inadequate to participate in it. He may appreciate the sensuality and tenderness it brings into his life, and he may very much want to participate fully, but he may be consciously or unconsciously unsure about his place. Because of his lack of preparedness he may feel inadequate in relating to the baby, and his own insecurities may be reinforced by the mother's anxiety about his capabilities at mothering. In her worry about his inexperience mother may unintentionally undercut his confidence. His feelings about having a daughter or having a son will inevitably influence his relationship to a new baby. And with a daughter, especially, he may feel in the dark about who she is, what to do with her, how to relate. With a boy child he can rely on his own experience of boyhood and maleness to aid him in building a relationship.

Father may feel excluded from the early mother-infant couple and become jealous. His relationship with his partner has changed with the entry of the third person, and his partner is no longer available to him in the same way. If the child is a girl, his feeling of being the "outsider" in the triangle may be increased. The closeness between mother and infant may also evoke happy or unsatisfactory experiences from his own infancy, when he was very close to a woman.

In our practice many women report having no real contact with their fathers. As adults they still wonder where father fits in their lives.[6] We often find that a daughter's relationship with father was not straightforward, that she experienced barriers and interceptions. The mother strongly affects the father-daughter relationship. A father's loving relationship with his daughter may cause friction, because mother may experience jealousy at his attention to daughter as well as anger because of what she feels is lacking in her life. Mother may feel that father shows gentle, caring affection to a daughter in ways he does not with her, and since her needy little-girl inside yearns for just this kind of attention, seeing it between her partner and their daughter can be painful. Mothers may unwittingly intercept this loving contact between a father and a daughter.

In addition, because father often spends very little time each day with a daughter, his availability to his daughter in those moments may stir up mother's resentment. She sees the child thrilled at father's attention and feels that all she gives is taken for granted or even negated. (She may also have a burden of unconscious jealousy: father's time at home used to be hers alone.)

These dynamics in the mother-father-daughter triangle are likely to be part of the girl's psychological development and they help explain why a daughter's relationship to her father is often undeveloped. Because she is so attuned to her mother, the daughter picks up mother's feelings, including any ambivalent feelings about daughter's relationship to father. The daughter may have to hide the contact she does have with him. As one woman put it, "Each time I phoned my parents I essentially talked to my mother. If my mother answered, then I never even had a word with my father. I would just tell my mother to send him my love. When my father answered the phone we talked for ten seconds, very superficially, and then my mother would come on the phone. When I became aware of this I tried to talk longer to my father and then my mother actually started picking up the extension."

Another dynamic we have consistently seen in our practice is that of a daughter's alliance with mother about father's inadequacies. Women often express contempt and disdain for their fathers because they are involved in mother's anger. Indeed, the daughter often carries her mother's rage. Women report feeling their fathers to be weak because they did not "stand up" to mother, especially in relation to them. "He wasn't strong enough to stop my mother's interceptions." "He didn't fight for a relationship with me." Once again daughter and mother share an experience. Both feel disappointed with father, both feel disdain, and thus they tighten their unspoken bond.

Father's position in the emotional triangle of the family is a critical piece in the puzzle of why it is so difficult for women to separate psychologically. The father-daughter relationship no more provides for unambiguous relating than the mother-daughter one does. Father is outside daughter's primary ambivalent relationship with mother but cannot offer an unambivalent one himself. Adolescence, then, the time of struggle toward independence, creates a psychic hiatus. Mother continues to relate in the push-pull while father is confronted with a daughter who is now a sexual being. This may well make him uncomfortable and as a result distant and inconsistent in his relating. Women who had good contact with their fathers and felt it changed dramatically during adolescence are likely to feel that there is something dangerous and wrong with their sexuality and that they are being punished because of it. The adolescent girl living in an emotional storm has no constant buoy.

The father-daughter relationship illustrates one of the tragedies of patriarchy. A man's position in the family and the significance of gender in his early psychological development means that he is often both ill prepared to give nurturance and afraid of women.[7] Men do not provide the emotional stability girls and women need either in their early struggles for psychological separation or in adult heterosexual relationships.

Father, then, stands at once outside the mother-daughter relationship and as the representative of the patriarchal order. Symbolically he represents for his daughter many things that are outside the world of women, the world of her mother, the world she is supposed to enter.

A daughter's psychology, then, is created in this nexus of family relations in a particular way. Like her mother before her, the woman's internal sense of self will be somewhat shaky and her psychological boundaries malleable.[8] She will have learned to hide her needy and would-be independent and initiating parts and will find herself searching in various ways for the missing connection in her life that will allow her the unambiguous nurturance she needs to continue her developmental task of separation. She will look to her husband and children to fill in the missing pieces, because the psychological merger with her mother thwarts her from achieving a solid sense of self and separateness. As a result she is well suited for her social role of handmaiden to others' activities. Her inner sense of unworthiness and unentitledness have been reinforced over and over again in the social constraints of her childhood and in the learning of her adult role. She has buried part of her self.

In the next chapter we shall explore the ways in which the hidden and unknown parts of a woman's psychology emerge in the context of a therapy situation.

Notes

1. Psychologists have observed this as part of "normal" development without considering the conditions that make this possible and the impact of mother-and-daughter psychology. For example, Winnicott, describing the mother's

ability to respond to her infant's needs in the first year of life, writes: "Towards the end of the pregnancy and for a few weeks after the birth of a child the mother is preoccupied with (or better 'given over to') the care of her baby, which at first seems like a part of herself; moreover she is very much identified with the baby and knows quite well what the baby is feeling like. For this she uses her own experience as a baby." (*Dependence Towards Independence: The Maturational Processes and the Facilitating Environment,* London, 1963.) He writes of the mother's primary maternal preoccupation as an "extraordinary condition which is almost like an illness. . . ." (*The Family and Individual Development,* London, 1965, pp. 15–16.) In the period when the mother is providing for the needs of the infant, and "finding the part of her that identifies with the infant, the mother is herself in a dependent state and vulnerable." (*The Maturational Processes and the Facilitating Environment,* London, 1963.)

2. Andrea Egan, who is doing a study on the experience of mothering, has informed us that many of the women she interviewed found that after the initial period of merger in infancy, as the baby turned more toward the world at six months of age, so mother had to readjust and redirect some of her interests outside her baby.

3. Nancy Friday, *My Mother, My Self,* New York, 1977.

4. Adrienne Rich, *Of Woman Born,* New York, 1976, p. 236.

5. From Freud's development of the concept of the Oedipus complex onward throughout psychoanalytic theory we see the analyst's attempt to incorporate the father as the central figure in psychological development. Freud himself recognized the critical nature of the early years of life for the girl's psychology and called this preoedipal—that is, he had to keep father in the picture and name everything else in relation to the father's entry into the world of the child. Even Melanie Klein could not abandon the father and so saw the oedipal conflict as happening in the first year of life.

6. Signe Hammer, *Passionate Attachments: Fathers and Daughters in America Today,* New York, 1982.

7. Men's psychology is obviously not the subject of this book, but for an explication of men's fear of women see Robert J. Stoller, *Sex and Gender,* New York, 1968, London, 1969; Dorothy Dinnerstein, *The Mermaid and the Minotaur: Sexual Arrangements and Human Malaise,* New York, 1976; and Luise Eichenbaum and Susie Orbach, *What Do Women Want? Exploding the Myth of Dependency,* New York, 1983.

8. Nancy Chodorow, *The Reproduction of Mothering: Psychoanalysis and the Sociology of Gender,* Berkeley, Calif. 1978; Jean Baker Miller, *Toward a New Psychology of Women,* Boston, Mass., 1976; and Carol Gilligan, *A Different Voice,* Cambridge, Mass., 1982. All have a more positive view of the developmental repercussions of women's malleable boundaries. They point to the certainty of affiliation in relating and the ways in which a feminine view of the world provides for safety and containment.

CHAPTER 3

The Feminist Psychotherapy Relationship-The Beginning Stage

We know ourselves as separate only in so far as we live in connection with others ... we experience relationships only in so far as we differentiate other from self.

CAROL GILLIGAN
In a Different Voice

PSYCHOANALYSIS and psychotherapy were developed in the nineteenth century as a treatment for mental distress. They were intended to help the individual who was suffering to experience herself or himself as living more fully in the world and less bounded by anxiety, depression, or hysterical symptoms. Freud developed his theories on the workings of the mind from the data he collected in his clinical practice. Using the technique of free association, he encouraged his analysands to speak freely and to tell their dreams. Thoughts and ideas that had been repressed revealed themselves in the analytic situation. Freud learned to read the unconscious material set out before him in a particular way, and these discoveries became the evidence for the picture he constructed of mental life.

Psychoanalytically oriented feminist therapy is also concerned with trying to understand the workings of the mind, with the aim of relieving the distressing symptoms that prevent a woman from feeling comfortable with and within herself. However, in our examination into the underlying causes of distress, we see the relationship between the intensely private, internal world—the psychic reality of the individual woman—and the external world, a patriarchal world that shapes her and within which she lives and develops. In our therapy we try to illuminate this internal world and reveal its profound influence on aspects of the woman's daily life. The therapy relationship provides the means to explore the structure of a woman's individual psyche, the workings of her unconscious, and her relational difficulties; and, of course, it facilitates the change that is desired and agreed upon.

Much of the psychological development theory we discuss in this book has come out of our observations of particular aspects of the therapy relationship itself, and this is how psychoanalytic theory has always been constructed: from practice to theory. In turn, all new theories of psychological development usher in changes in the actual practice of psychoanalytic therapy. As the theory develops, it refines aspects of the practice, and these tried-out interventions in turn further refine the theory. Here we will propose theory, based on our observations and work, about the practice of a feminist-oriented psychoanalytical therapy, because we anticipate that certain kinds of issues will be central to the therapeutic work and the shape of the therapy relationship. We have observed that particular issues arise within that relationship, and we think our understanding of the construction of femininity, especially the centrality of the mother-daughter relationship, has implications for the process toward such therapeutic tasks as separation and autonomy.

The therapeutic situation allows for a unique kind of relationship, in which the client's subjective conscious and unconscious experience is central and the most minute details and traces of experiences are explored and investigated. Therapy involves painstaking attention to nuance, to emphasis, to emotional blocks, to fantasies, to the links between thoughts and feelings.

The process itself centers on two features: one is the actual content—what therapists call the material—that the client discusses with the therapist. This material includes anxieties, fantasies, problems within relationships, problems within oneself, problems with work. The second feature is the relationship between two people engaged in psychotherapy together, the client and the therapist. Classical psychoanalysis holds that there is both a transference relationship and a reality relationship between client and therapist.[1] Transference is not a very complicated concept and can often be seen in everyday life. It is the phenomenon of bringing one's emotional responses from the past, the ones we acquired in childhood, into present-day relationships and situations. We bring who we are into all relationships, and transference means that we are assigning—that is transferring—the feelings, attitudes, and behaviors that make up who we were, but also the feelings and behaviors and attitudes that we now have toward other people that originated in our relations to others from infancy. Transference occurs frequently in everyday adult life, but its manifestations are often cut short by the actual responses of others, who do not necessarily fit into one's internal scheme and in one way or another do not take on the transference. New relationships can challenge deeply held emotional pictures, but new relationships can also repeat old patterns and thereby confirm old ways of relating.

The psychotherapeutic situation provides a place for examination of the origin and persistence of transference feelings that may arise in the client in relation to the therapist.

They give us information about the client's inner life and motivations.

Freud used his observations of transference relationships with his patients in building his theory of psychological development, and classical psychoanalysis in general sees transference as originating in the repetition compulsion, which causes a person to continually reenact a form of behavior in an effort to come to grips with it. Transference feelings belong to significant figures, usually parents, from the past; the feelings are now displaced and projected onto the therapist. Thus in classical theory transference to the analyst was inevitably understood in libidinal terms, with the analyst representing the longed-for oedipal parent.

Modern developments in psychodynamic therapy have shifted from interpreting the transference relationship as an expression of the nonresolution of the Oedipus complex to a much earlier development stage, from which the individual brings to therapy a distilled picture of her or his early relationships with others (that is, her or his internal object relations). For Balint, Winnicott, Klein, and Guntrip the therapy relationship revealed the difficulties in patterns of very early relating. In this sense they did not see themselves as the oedipal parent but as the maternal object.[2] For many modern theorists it is this pre-oedipal period that is crucial in the formation of psychic structure. In therapy and within the transference relationship the therapist works toward an understanding of the client's experience of the external world in terms of her or his object relations.

A feminist view of transference can incorporate both classical and modern views. We draw on the information we gather from what is happening between the therapist and the person in therapy to build our theory about women's psychological development. Uncovering the dynamics of the mother-daughter relationship within the therapy provides an

understanding of the steps of feminine personality development. From our perspective the most critical relationship
that is going to come up in the transference is that between
mother and daughter. This prediction is based on our experiences of working directly with women and supervising the
case load of other therapists working with them. This will
not always be the first thing that is talked about in therapy
or that is immediately obvious in the transference relationship, but sooner or later it will be addressed at great length
during the course of therapy.

As we will detail, the critical work in therapy devolves in
the real relationship between the two people doing therapy
together. In our view *this* relationship is central to the reparative work. The two women[3] in the room are relating to
each other, and although many resonances of past relationships will be worked on and used in the therapy, there is also
a new, real relationship developing between these two. We
see this new relationship as an extremely powerful event in
the life of the woman client. It may well be the first time she
has been in a situation in which the acknowledged purpose
of the relationship is for her to get help from another woman. This in itself resonates with her early desires and evokes
longing, guilt, and conflict at the same time that it opens up
new doors and possibilities about being given to, being addressed, and learning to receive.

The Beginning Stage of Therapy

Let us look closely at the beginning of the therapy relationship, when a woman client and a woman therapist meet
for the first time. For the client this is a big step and an

72

extremely sensitive time. She has been able to admit to herself and another person that she needs help, although at this point she may not be able to put into words what her problems are. The client brings her distress, her need and desire to be helped, together with her fear, nervousness, and anxiety, and tries to explain to her therapist what her problem—often called the "presenting problem"—is.

The therapist as one half of the therapy relationship has three tasks at this stage. First, she must be able to empathize with the initial concerns of the client, and convey this by her manner. Many women feel extremely vulnerable entering therapy, and many feel unsure of what to say or do.[4] It is the therapist's responsibility to provide shaping and certain boundaries, so that the woman can gradually come to feel safe.

Second, the therapist has to provide concrete information about the therapy—fees, time of appointments, and such specific information. She may need to explain a bit about the process of therapy, and she should talk about her theoretical biases so that the client knows what kind of therapy she is committing herself to. Obviously this should be done with tact and sensitivity: no two clients and no two therapy relationships are the same. One woman may want to know quite a lot about the therapist's background, while another would feel overloaded or bombarded with such information. When possible the therapist will also need to discuss treatment goals and methods, since, for example, it is most disconcerting for a woman to enter therapy with anxiety about a specific presenting problem—such as a phobia—only to discover months later that the therapist's view of a useful treatment model is to remove the emphasis from direct discussion of the phobia.

Third, through the first months of therapy, especially, the

therapist must work hard to provide a context within which the client can open up. She must listen very carefully to what her client is saying on several levels, try to understand what the client's experience is and feel what the client is feeling. Painful as it may sometimes be, she needs to feel herself in her client's shoes. A good therapist may come out of a session with strong feelings which, when analyzed, she can see have been transmitted to her by the client.

In the beginning stages of therapy the client will probably be talking about a particular situation she has just experienced or is currently experiencing. The therapist is listening, trying to understand, and help the client understand, what that experience means for her. She is giving to her client in an immediate way by showing her concern and at the same time trying to clarify with the client what she is actually saying and experiencing. She does this in a very straightforward way, summarizing the main points, asking about the emotional sparks coming from the client, or elucidating what she sees as the particular area of conflict or upset. From the start the therapist is creating a language for a dialogue with the client's inner world, to help the client feel less isolated in her pain. The experience of being understood is starting, for in our therapy we make an assumption that the woman has rarely felt herself to be accurately heard or understood, that she has not had the opportunity to describe in detail the complexities of her psychological experience. Much of her energy will have gone toward helping others understand their experiences. She will have known herself in that role and developed a certain comfort with it. She will also, most probably, have derived a certain amount of self-esteem from knowing that she has a good ear, is understanding, patient, and concerned with others. Now the focus is on her. An essential part of the therapy lies in building a relationship in which the structure and purpose is radically different. The therapist needs to indicate her willingness and her availability to the client, so the woman can have a reasonable expectation of being heard and understood. The interventions that the therapist makes—questions, interpretations, or clarifications—are the means by which the therapist communicates her receptivity and availability to the client.

At the same time the therapist is absorbing information about the client's psychology. She is drawing out the underlying issues and sketching the psychology of the woman in order to be able to work with and help her. The client is talking about a particular situation and the therapist is trying to help with it, but she is also using its wider ramifications to build up a picture of the client's particular psychology.

For example, Rosalyn came to her first therapy appointment distraught and desperate after the breakup of a long relationship. As she talked about her pain, she showed a kind of resignation, subtly indicating that this was going to be her pattern, she couldn't hope for more. This was what was in the cards for her. She had always known somehow that she and Alan would split up, and she had lived for a year in the grip of agonizing jealousy over a woman friend of theirs. Knowing that Alan liked the woman, Rosalyn had imagined that the two were longing to go off together. In that first session Rosalyn showed that she both idealized Alan and utterly denigrated him. She had always felt terribly insecure with him and had never been able to trust him. She talked in a very agitated way, frantically attempting to turn Alan's rather noncommittal recent statements into evidence that he wanted to revive their love affair. She couldn't bear to know it was over.

As the therapist hears all that Rosalyn is saying, she is wondering why Rosalyn can't accept the ending of the relationship. She is aware of Rosalyn's anxiety and desperation and notes that very little direct feeling is able to come through at the moment. It is as though Rosalyn is shrieking *no, no, no.* The therapist is alerted to the twin issues of loss and attachment. She is interested in the images Rosalyn has of Alan. She notices that Rosalyn felt insecure in the relationship but feels lost without it. She wonders about the reality of the "other woman" and Rosalyn's feeling of betrayal by two people so close to her. She notices that Rosalyn talks of them both in the same way, and she wonders whether the agitation—the "buzzing"—isn't perhaps covering an extremely painful set of feelings involving rejection, betrayal, and despair about being loved properly. In these early meetings she is tentatively sketching a developmental picture, a picture of Rosalyn's internal object relations.

The therapist is experiencing the client in this beginning relationship. She is alert to how the client presents herself— how she sits, how she communicates her emotions, where there are obvious blocks, the way she enters the room, and how she affects the therapist. The therapist is also aware of the impact a particular session has on her. If she feels sad after a session, she needs to think about her sadness in relation to what her client was sharing with her. During the session the client may have told of something sad but related it with no affect (Rosalyn could not show her inner feelings), in quite an unemotional way, so that the therapist ended up carrying the emotion for her.

Here as always, what the therapist feels after a session is very useful in the beginning stages of therapy. It is often a communication from the client, in this case one who is not able to feel her own sadness because she is frightened by the open expression of sad feelings, which she has learned to consider awkward and immature. (What the therapist feels in response to the client's spoken and unspoken communication is called countertransference.[5])

The therapist also takes in the changes during the session—its quality, its texture, the way the client's feelings change—and she notices what happens at the end of the session, how the client leaves her. She is aware of the ways in which the client keeps or misses appointments, whether she is habitually on time, late, or early. All these details, the very guts of the therapy process, are looked at and thought about, because they reveal how the client's inner world is expressed in this relationship, and they contribute to the larger picture that will be developed over the course of the therapy, the full picture of who the client is and what the therapy relationship will be.

In the early stages of therapy the therapist tries to build a sense of trust so that the therapy can proceed, but the development of trust is very complicated. Very often a major reason for seeking therapy turns out to be difficulty in trusting. The therapy process is about being understood and heard, feeling that another is really interested and concerned, making an emotional connection that helps dissolve the defenses that prevent one from trusting. When we use the word *trusting* in the context of the initial stages of therapy, however, it has a more limited meaning and simply connotes the possibilities that exist in the situation. Many clients do not know what is supposed to happen in therapy. At the same time they feel the need for help they are worried about what is expected of them and how to go about being "in therapy." In these early sessions it is important for the therapist to give some reassuring information about the process of therapy— for example, that it is a relationship between the two people in the room; that it will take time for the therapist to understand the client but that is what she wants to do and what she is there for. The therapist also needs to provide the client with new ways of looking at her experience and at who she is, and to reassure her that the ways of being and coping she has used in the past can be rejected if they are no longer helpful. What the therapist is providing for her client is the possibility of change.

At this stage the therapist is likely to be the potential lifeline or anchor for the client. *Potential* is the right word because at the beginning of therapy the client is protecting herself. She is cautious; she is taking stock of her therapist; she is not necessarily making an immediate link. She may be acutely embarrassed about finding herself there in the first place. She has hopes and expectations but she is also self-protective. Consciously and unconsciously she is asking, "Will this person actually be able to help me, will she be able to understand who I am? Can I be helped or is it all hopeless? Dare I open myself up to this person, dare I bring my needs into this relationship; am I going to be disappointed?"

These doubts and questions can take subtle forms. They are defense mechanisms in the client's struggle not to feel pain, anger, loss—unpleasant feelings that can be very frightening. Defense mechanisms operate in self-destructive as well as self-protective ways, for as the defense attempts to keep out rejections and disappointments from the outside world, it can simultaneously prevent care and nurturance from coming in. So the hidden part of the psyche develops defenses to protect it from anticipated hurt.

Defenses also protect others, loved and needed people, from the person's hidden self which may be felt to be destructive, devouring, or bad. Defenses may push people away or keep them at a distance, and possibly aid in the development of unsatisfactory relationships which only reinforce the anticipated fear of rejection or the feeling that it is impossible to have contact in a relationship. The therapist will experience the same kind of defense mechanisms that the client has developed in her other relationships, and it is important to remember that they have been developed in the first place as protection in distressing situations.

In one sense defenses are creative mechanisms for psychological protection. Defenses create distance and separateness from others. They are psychological adaptations arising out of fear and upset; they are used to build a defensive stance in relation to the world. They create a smokescreen to protect the deep inner needs that a person fears cannot be met.

In the first years of life the psychological birth of the human infant entails the experience of contact and the taking in of nurturance from the caregiver. This complex relationship contains enormous pleasure, intimacy, and sensuality as well as upset, frustration, distance, and difficulty. As the psyche is developing it copes with the difficult aspects of this relationship by splitting them off and thus creating defenses against the distressing experiences. A woman with a particularly deprived relationship with her mother may, for example, say at the beginning of therapy that she does not want or expect anything from her mother. Her attempt at not wanting, and at appearing to others as not wanting, turns out to be a defense against its very opposite, her tremendous feelings of neediness and yearning for nurturance from her mother.

As people develop through childhood to adulthood, their defenses may become entrenched. The aim in psychoanalysis is to help individuals recognize their personal defenses and thereby get through to the feelings, the fears, and the developmental blocks in which they are trapped.

Different schools of psychoanalysis have specific ways of

interpreting defenses.[6] One view is that from the very beginning the therapist should interpret these defenses and analyze them for the client. This can be done in two ways: interpreting defenses that the client has outside therapy—in a situation with a friend, a lover, or a co-worker, for instance—or interpreting the defenses that the client brings into the therapy relationship. Our view is that precisely because the client comes into the therapy room feeling vulnerable, it is important that her vulnerability not be exposed to the extent that she feels helpless. We follow the client's initiatives and try to understand what seems important and central to her, intervening to help us both get a fuller picture of any specific situation but not "pouncing on" the defenses at the outset. We see the importance of offering interpretations about defenses that may be operating both outside the therapy and in the therapy relationship. But for us the interpretation of the defenses is not the sine qua non of the therapist's role but a communication within the therapy relationship, a bridge to understanding.

We see defense mechanisms, then, as operating on two levels. Defenses may be psychological mechanisms that push people away, keep people at a distance, and even help develop bad relationships. On the other hand, defenses have been constructed as a protection. They came from difficult dynamics in central relationships in the first place and developed as an imperfect but workable response to hurt, rejection, loss, pain, and anger. It is in this sense that we say defenses are creative mechanisms with which human beings protect themselves in the world.

We think it is important to acknowledge both aspects of a particular defense. In our experience any sort of attack or criticism of the defense strengthens it, frightening the client because she feels that something she still needs is going to be taken away from her. As therapists we do not always know at the outset what a client's particular defense is. We may notice a certain reluctance or edginess in exploring a particular issue and this will alert us to how difficult an issue this is for the client. But in our practice we have found that it is only through the therapist's acceptance of the defenses as a part of the therapy relationship that progress is made. The therapist has to somehow peek behind the defense to see what the client is trying to express. She must not be put off by the defenses but must be alert to them. She then shares her awareness with the client, so that the defenses are not ignored but are an acknowledged aspect of the relationship. She provides the sense that the relationship is a safe place for the client, so that what the defenses are protecting can slowly emerge. This acceptance of defenses by the therapist enables the two people slowly to come to look at and recognize the defenses together. References to them become part of the language that therapist and client share.

This process was highlighted in working with Roberta, a twenty-eight-year-old statistician who had been suffering from anorexia nervosa for ten years. She weighed very little and restricted herself to one low-fat yogurt and an apple a day. Roberta spent some of each session talking about how much she had eaten and reiterating her notion that she mustn't get fatter. She wanted to tell the therapist how much smaller she would like to be and how awful she felt at having eaten at all. Since these concerns were uppermost in Roberta's mind, the main content of her defense, they needed to be directly investigated. At the same time the therapist was trying to relate to the Roberta who was behind the defense and barely visible, the vulnerable and scared person whom the defense was trying to protect. In such a situation the therapist needs to understand the importance of the defense, the strength it demonstrates, and the necessary if transitory self-esteem it gives the client. Only when a client feels trust, safety, and security within the therapy relationship will the defenses dissolve.

In the beginning stage of therapy one may well share this process with the client. The therapist may indicate that as the client begins to feel met and understood in the relationship, the defenses will dissolve because she will begin to find new ways of being herself. Roberta and the therapist together will come to see the psychic dilemma that Roberta's anorexia, her essential defense mechanism, is straddling. It is a method for feeling good about herself that Roberta depends on in the absence of a secure internal sense of self.

Our theory of the psychic structural development of women suggests that the defenses we encounter in the therapy relationship can be understood this way: The defenses are protecting the little-girl inside who is hidden away from the world. This little-girl inside can feel as if she is the authentic part of the person, the "whole" of the adult woman, but the woman is likely to feel that her little-girl self is unattractive, dangerous, unlovable. She therefore feels that *she* is unattractive, dangerous, unlovable. She fears that what she wants and who she is will be rejected. The defenses are thus operating on two levels. First, they are protecting the little-girl inside from anticipated hurt and rejection. Second, they are meant to protect those very others from seeing the little-girl inside. The woman feels this aspect of herself to be so ugly, unlovable, violent, needy, and insistent that once out in the open it will take over, pushing away those it needs so much from. An unconscious internal calculation ensues: Better not to reveal anything that would risk engendering rejection. Concentrate instead on pleasing others. Then one does not have to address one's own unseemly needs directly.

Jane, for example, had a confusing set of reactions to a

family party. When her mother and brother planned her father's seventieth birthday celebration, she was not consulted on her ideas and was not asked to take any responsibility. Her name was not even included on the party invitation, which listed her mother, her brother, and her sister-in-law as hosts. She was hurt and angry at being ignored, and this put her in touch with her little-girl part, but these conscious feelings passed quickly and on the surface Jane was aware of feeling upset and confused. Why had she been excluded? They must have forgotten her. As we talked in therapy Jane put forward the idea that her desire to be included was all wrong. She had been out of the country when the party was planned and she could understand why she had been left out. She couldn't ask her mother or brother about their decision because she couldn't bear to find out that she wasn't that important. Another good reason not to ask was that she might show her anger to her family, from whom she still felt she needed recognition.

Jane, like all women we have met in therapy, needs to expose her little-girl inside to the therapist, although she will not be aware of this in the early stages of therapy. This inner self needs to emerge so that it can be nurtured and responded to by the therapist. The woman needs to have a different experience in the new relationship but the hidden part of herself is scared that the interaction will not be successful, that she will be rejected once again. The defenses within the therapy may well work to present an image to the therapist of a woman who does not have many needs and will not overburden the therapist.[7]

So the little-girl inside the woman comes into the therapy room with her full set of defenses and protections against dependency desires, both those she feels now and those she has felt throughout her life. The woman may feel tremendous guilt and shame about such desires and try to push them away, condemning herself for having such feelings. Even if she cannot articulate what they are, she inevitably feels that it is inappropriate to have such needs and to want them understood and satisfied by the therapist. If she talks about her needs at all, she tends to denigrate herself in anticipation of criticism from the therapist, openly or indirectly. Thus at the beginning of therapy the therapist must reassure the client that it is acceptable to express dependency desires and must encourage her to explore her wishes. Together the two can help relieve the client of the guilt that imprisons these feelings.

The freeing of these feelings, the exploration of their meaning, and finding ways to satisfy them are a major focus in the middle and most prolonged stage of the therapy relationship.

Notes

1. For a summary of contemporary positions on transference, countertransference, and the therapy relationship, see J. Sandler, C. Dare, and A. Holden, *The Patient and the Analyst,* London, 1973.

2. It is interesting that none of Freud's successors were able to jettison the Oedipus complex, although their work clearly demonstrates what could be achieved by examining early object relations. They are all careful to reassure us that their work in no way replaces Freud's but concentrates rather on his studies of earlier psychological development.

3. We are describing our practice at The Women's Therapy Centre, where the relationship has been that of two women. This raises the interesting point that has been put to use a number of times about whether a man can be a feminist therapist and provide this reparative relationship for a woman in therapy. Our own position on this is that it is possible for a man to work out of a feminist understanding and to concentrate on the mother-daughter aspects of the transference relationship and the difficulties that face a woman. A discussion of gender would need to run through the therapy so that the meaning of the male therapist as nurturer could be understood at all its various levels.

4. In our training sessions we are often led to remind therapists to reflect on the way they felt when they first sought therapy, to sensitize them to the kind

of state their new client may be in. This seems to be necessary because a great deal of training encourages a particular kind of distance between the therapist and the client. This can lead to an unfortunate "us" and "them" situation. For example, we have heard therapists complain that a new client asked a lot of inappropriate questions in the first session; they have forgotten that as yet the client does not know what to say or do or how to go about it. Therapists obviously become extremely practiced about operating in the therapy relationship, and they can forget how well they have ingested its rules. A therapist, for example, is used to silences and will not be alarmed or agitated if the room is quiet for five minutes. A client, however, may be confused or anxious, because normal social intercourse rarely includes such silences. The client may not know that they are all right and useful in this context as a time of reflection and evocation of feelings.

5. See note 1, page 136, for an explanation of our use of the concept of countertransference.

6. In some schools an interpretation of a defense can sound like an attack. We do not share this approach. For example, a client meets a therapist for the first time; the therapist knows nothing of the client and the client knows nothing of the therapist. The analyst believes the client should come for psychoanalysis or psychotherapy at least three times a week. The client, who knows very little about therapy at this point, says, "Well, actually, I was thinking more of coming once a week; I thought that was what therapy was about," and she may add, "That's all that I can afford." The therapist interprets this as a defense and says, "I think you may be afraid of letting yourself open up to me. You don't want to help yourself, you're afraid to let yourself get well." This example shows how something can be interpreted as a defense which may not be one at all, because the client may just not know of the "unwritten rules" about how often to come to therapy. If we believed that in this case therapy three times a week was very important, we would discuss with the client why we thought so and have a dialogue about how she felt about coming to therapy once, twice, or three times a week. The important thing would be for the client to have the choice. The client is half of the therapy relationship. We should respect her power and her impact within the relationship throughout the therapy, and especially at the beginning. For instance, we might say, "Well, why don't we start once a week and see how it goes, and discuss coming more times a week as we go along?" If coming once a week was indeed some sort of protection or defense, we would store this information about the client and share it with her at a later date if it reflected other aspects of her personality and could be useful to her.

7. A feminist analysis is really central here to guide us in our work with women. It is easy to see that if one does not work with an awareness of the meaning of socialization to the feminine gender, one could be tempted to take such an attitude at face value, thus unconsciously colluding with the client in continuing to hide her needs. (This will be a theme throughout the therapy. As the needs are revealed the client will experience discomfort. After all, who is actually used to seeing or hearing about women's needs?)

CHAPTER 4

The Feminist Psychotherapy Relationship- The Middle Stage and Separating

The Middle Stage

The middle stage of therapy lasts anywhere from six months to five or six years. By now a relationship between client and therapist has been established. There is a basis of trust. The therapist has provided concrete help for the client in dealing with different aspects of her life and understanding herself better in all kinds of situations. Together they have built a shared language and understanding—a way of looking at and expressing what is happening in the client's internal world.

A central issue during this entire middle stage of therapy is dependency, which involves the woman's struggle with her dependency needs in all relationships, including the therapy relationship. Women are thought of as dependent people. Dependency is associated with qualities such as clinging, helplessness, and weakness. Women have been put in a position of being economically dependent within patriarchy,

86

but the relationship between economic dependency and emotional dependency is not straightforward.[1] Although this is not usually made explicit within the relationship, men's dependency needs are most often met within marriage and their emotional worries are processed by their wives. No equivalent place exists for women. Women learn quite early not to expect this kind of nurturance from a woman or a man, and so they come to protect themselves from their dependency needs.

Dependency feelings are terribly painful for a woman because they force awareness of her needs, which in turn, because they are not being met, reinforce her feelings of unworthiness and emptiness. The picture she must present to the world is of an adult woman, but inside she feels like a child, and her feelings of dependency painfully confirm her smallness. The tension between women and men in heterosexual relationships often centers on this dynamic, with women alternately curbing and exposing their dependency needs and men being perplexed, angered, or intimidated by them. (This becomes especially apparent in couple counseling, which is discussed in chapter 9.) As we look into this dynamic, a picture unfolds of both women and men being wary of women's dependency needs and consciously and unconsciously working together to suppress them.

In the clinical situation women reveal how they defend against such needs. Often they have created a protective boundary between themselves and those to whom they wish to relate closely, and they express fear that if the little-girl emerges within intimate relationships then they will become only the little-girl. The woman's shaky boundaries lead her to feel that somehow she will lose herself and be taken over, subsumed in the other person. Or she may feel that the little-girl inside will take over the other person if she is released at all. Women carry with them the feeling that their needs are overwhelming, unending, insatiable, bad, shameful. They feel their needs will drive other people away; many women say with distressing positiveness that they will be rejected because of this needy part of themselves.

Veronica had been involved in an "on-again-off-again" love affair for several years. She enjoyed being really close to Larry, her lover, and didn't understand why things went wrong so regularly. Larry was also very committed to Veronica. During the course of therapy it became clear that Veronica had a habit of breaking off with Larry after vacations, which they spent together very happily. (These vacations usually coincided with the therapist's vacation.) Typically in the spring and fall Larry would plan to start various projects, such as carpentry class or fencing, which Veronica saw as taking him away from the relationship. She unconsciously translated this in the following way: Larry had felt burdened at spending so much time with her but couldn't say so. His involvement in such activities was both proof and punishment that she had overstepped the mark in terms of showing her needs. Feeling that Larry would not be available to her any more, and not wishing to be humiliated by being clingy, Veronica withdrew first by suggesting a short separation. She had a terribly difficult time recognizing her need for Larry, and she couldn't enjoy being close with him without fearing that the closeness would be taken away. Even though Larry was never the one to initiate a breakup she couldn't trust that he would really be there for her or that it was all right for her to rely on their closeness and intimacy. She was so afraid of disappointment that she imagined rejections and then withdrew before they could occur, thus delivering a rejection herself.

This happens in the therapy relationship as well. At one

level we see an adult woman; but our therapy alerts us to the little-girl inside the woman, together with all the defenses that hide her. It is this little-girl who emerges time and time again, albeit with tremendous hesitancy, with woman after woman, in every therapy relationship we have experienced. Since most women do not feel good about this little-girl inside, their critical view of her will be reflected in the judgmental way they describe their feelings. The woman feels that the therapist will reject the little-girl, so she cannot expose her. There is a step-by-step process whereby the therapist responds to this little-girl behind the defenses, encourages her to come out into the relationship, and reassures the client that the therapist will not be overwhelmed by this little-girl, is not afraid of her, and does not feel that this part of the woman is bad, greedy, and ugly. The client reacts in two ways during this process. She feels tremendous potential: here at last is someone who may not reject her, who may really accept her, someone who may be able to respond to all these feelings that she has had so much difficulty with herself. At the same time she is still cautious, because to let the little-girl out openly within the therapy relationship and thus admit to being close to and needing the therapist is an acknowledgment of dependency on another person.

Veronica, for example, felt very uncomfortable about showing her therapist how important she was. She didn't like to acknowledge that there was a link between her breaking up with Larry and the therapist's return from vacation. As her therapy proceeded Veronica felt that being in two important—that is, dependent—relationships simultaneously was something she could handle as long as it wasn't made explicit that she needed both the therapist and Larry. When she was brought face to face with those needs she felt ashamed and, as she put it, "greedy." In the summer she would banish the therapist from her conscious mind and allow herself to be close to her lover. In the fall, with the therapist's return, she would drop Larry and come back to therapy full of anger at his projects. In this way she protected herself from the knowledge of her dependency and at the same time tried to protect the therapist from her feelings of anger, disappointment, and despair that arose at having to face the issue.

Why are these feelings of dependency so terrifying? Why do they make women feel so vulnerable and insecure? To find the answer we need to look at the context in which women's psyches develop. In our very first relationship, the one we all had, we were totally dependent for our physical and emotional growth. In the first months of life, as the ego is in the process of forming, there is not yet a sense of self. This state of helplessness and dependency, together with the original infantile state of early ego formation, is carried deep within our memory. This was a time when we were merged psychologically with mother and did not yet have any sense of our own or other people's boundaries. This sense of self gradually develops and emerges through the relationship the baby has with those around it.

As a female infant develops, the mother tends to identify with her and, because of her feelings about herself and her little-girl inside, transmits both a positive and a negative sense of self. Mother's complex feelings about her own, and in turn her daughter's emotional dependency needs create the push-pull between mother and daughter. When the little daughter comes to feel that her emotional dependency needs are not acceptable, a split occurs and her dependent little-girl self is hidden. The split results in further deprivation for that little-girl inside, because she is not in contact with others, not receiving the nurture and love that are necessary for continued growth.

Then comes that second "push" for the little girl, when she has to try to give up her mother as her primary love object and to turn her interest and expectation toward her father, the embodiment of all males, to achieve successful heterosexual socialization and sexual orientation. She experiences both of these "pushes" as rejection by mother. Central to the issue of women's dependency, then, is the effect of the push-pull dynamic. Deeply buried inside a woman's psychology is the feeling that her dependency needs—and therefore *herself*—are not acceptable, that they will be met with rejection and she will be pushed away yet again.

The woman brings all these feelings about her little-girl self into the relationship with her therapist. Women clients find it painful to acknowledge their feelings of deprivation and consequent neediness, and they often fight to hide their fear that the therapist will not be able to accept and meet their needs. But a cornerstone for us of feminist therapy is the determination to bring this conflict into the open, for as it is gradually exposed the woman will come to understand more about what it is she searches for in her relationships.

These dependency needs are central to the therapeutic relationship, and the therapist's job is to encourage the client to express them.[2] Women frequently say that in intimate relationships they yearn for someone who will provide a climate of emotional security and at the same time allow them to remain individuals, their own persons. Because one of a woman's unconscious fears is that she will lose herself and become merged with her partner, and because she does not believe that anyone could allow her to be both close *and separate*, the issue of dependency is conflictual.

In this middle phase of therapy, the therapist is trying to confirm and help strengthen this desire to be both close and separate. She does this by appreciating who the client is and what she wants. When the woman was little, part of the reason the separation from mother was particularly problematic was that mother, lacking a separate sense of self, could not withdraw sufficiently from the merged state to be able to help her daughter name and authenticate her experience. She read her daughter's signals as best she could, but her own repressed inner needs found expression in the way she saw what was going on for her daughter. The push-pull dynamic we have seen in relation to a daughter's dependency needs is also present in her other needs, such as self-actualization and autonomy. These are as much taboos for women as are the open expression of dependency needs (as distinct from dependency behavior, which women are encouraged to exhibit. Dependency behaviors such as displaying physical weakness, or the lack of understanding of "complicated," unfamiliar phenomena such as accounting or car mechanics, are ways in which women attempt to get taken care of.) These initiatives are related to in staccato fashion, which is the reason why girls have complicated feelings about doing things, being experimental, and going full steam ahead for what they want.

Part of the therapist's job is to nourish these initiating parts, to encourage the client to find out what she wants and to work through the intrapsychic barriers such as guilt, illegitimacy, and hopelessness that make it hard for her to feel comfortable about knowing what she wants and taking steps to fulfill her desires. Here too a feminist sensibility means that the therapist can avoid certain pitfalls. One anticipates that initiating activities are problematic, that this very fact causes shame because it is related to complexities of betrayal and guilt in the mother-daughter relationship: "How can I go after what my mother didn't have?" It is not simply a question of providing tools for assertion, useful though these may be. The therapist needs to help the client identify the undergrowth that makes it so terribly hard for her to first know what she wants and then feel all right about wanting and getting. These psychic barriers need to be explored time and time again in the course of therapy, because the problems do not get worked through easily.

In being close and separate—that is, by showing genuine interest and concern without losing her boundaries—the therapist is providing the kind of relationship the client wants. Her needs for closeness are met without sacrifice of autonomy. In the transferential aspects of the relationship, client and therapist sort through the difficulties the client has in receiving this care and attention and actually believing that such needs can be met. As they face together how the woman's needs have been inappropriately responded to before, they create a model (which the client will use with the constraints of therapy removed and with more mutuality) for a new kind of relating that is both close and separate. This will influence the woman's subsequent intimate relationships just as the early mother-daughter interactions shaped so much of her previous relating.

As the therapy proceeds, and the neediness (as well as gratitude for being related to) is expressed in the relationship, we discover that many women feel the urge to take care of the therapist. At the point of being able to take in the therapist's caring, the woman may become caught up in worrying and fantasizing about the needs of the therapist. By exploring this dynamic in the transference relationship, we discover another critical component of the mother-daughter relationship. When the client takes in good feelings from another woman, she is experiencing an unusual emotional state. This may both please her and make her anxious. She may feel frightened that she will lose this new kind of caring and attempt to mobilize against her anxiety by taking care of the therapist. She may feel she needs to take care of the therapist in order to keep her there. Women remember doing this with their mothers even in childhood, and they remember their mothers looking after their grandmothers. To keep mother close to her, a woman will become her mother's mother—and mother may have encouraged this out of her own need to be looked after.

Precisely because the client's life history has not prepared her to receive caring from another woman on a consistent basis, she may find this situation hard to negotiate psychically. She may find herself involved in a series of what might be called tests, ways of coping with the contact in this relationship. She may express her fears by worrying about whether the therapist will understand her or will disappoint her. If the therapist can look at such tests from this vantage point, it is easier not to become embroiled in them.[3] The therapist, who anticipates that the new sense of contact is bound to bring its own difficulties, is less likely to play into them or feel offended. Nevertheless, this can be a difficult transitional period for the therapist. Having worked so hard with the client to reach this stage, she may now experience frustration and confusion. But if she is alert to the fact that her client may (unconsciously) need to call on her defenses, she will be able to help them both get through this period by looking at what happened in the contact—helping the client address why this very contact was so hard and exactly what it felt like—rather than pushing away in return. This kind of approach to misunderstanding or disappointment helps clarify the underlying difficulties around the issue of contact, so that the client can consolidate some of the changes she has been working so hard to achieve.

When real cases of disappointment arise in the therapy relationship, as they are bound to, they have to be examined in their reality. The therapist must be able to explore with the client what this disappointment means: Can the client accept that somebody with whom she has a relationship, who is giving to her, may disappoint, may make mistakes? The therapist must unravel the basic issue and establish whether or not this disappointment is a defense against the client's growing belief that the therapist is truly with her.

The issue of disappointment in the therapeutic relationship brings women therapists and their clients up against the image of women that most of us, and men too, carry deep inside; women are felt to be either all-good and all-providing or all-withholding and disappointing. When a client feels disappointed with the therapist, both she and the therapist may fall prey to this image of women as inadequate. We discussed earlier the time in a girl's life when she builds a world of internal relationships which are more manageable than those in the exterior world. She takes into herself two pictures of how mother could be, seeing her as someone who has the capacity to make everything all right but who also withholds. These two images are not just pictures of mother. Because of the process of internalization they form a basic sense of the little girl's identity and who she will be as a grown woman.[4] In a transferential way, all women take on this dual aspect in the girl's inner world. All women then embody the capacity to give or to betray, and women approach other women with these unconscious images, simultaneously hoping to find nurturance and yet sure they will be disappointed.

These contradictory images are also projected onto a female therapist, whom the client is likely to experience as all-providing or all-withholding. When Jane's therapist forgot a detail of a story Jane had told her, Jane felt stopped in her tracks, frozen; it was as though the therapist had "turned into a witch." The therapist had the job of acknowledging that she had indeed disappointed Jane, and this opened the way for them to work out together how and why Jane had so readily transformed the therapist into a witch. It is most important within the context of this relationship between the two women for them to reject the image of the therapist as either all-powerful or all-terrible and acknowledge instead that the therapist may sometimes disappoint, but that this does not transform her ability to also give.

Alongside the process of the woman client bringing her little-girl self into the therapy and unraveling her defenses runs another, equally important process, that may be called the repair work. When we described the early psychological development of the infant girl, we discussed how she takes in the person of the mother, embodies it, and in turn creates herself. We observed how child-rearing arrangements in which women do all the mothering can make it hard for a woman to move into and then out of a merged state with her developing child, and how as a result the girl may feel somewhat confused about her own self-boundaries.

All the women we have seen in therapy have come with problems and confusions about their sense of self because they did not embody enough of mother to allow them to separate. As this aspect of a woman's psychology emerges in therapy, the wish to merge, to be closely connected to the therapist—as well as the anxiety this arouses—is a subtext running through the relationship. The therapist is aware of the ways in which the early nurturance was inconsistent, and in being consistent herself she offers a new kind of psychological umbilical cord. She creates a circle of care and attentiveness that surrounds the therapy relationship. She provides a sense of containment, what Winnicott called a "holding environment," in which the still needy little-girl inside is now nurtured in the emotional contact with the therapist.[5]

Being respected and related to precisely and rhythmically,

the woman slowly lets down her defenses as she begins to feel the care of the therapist. Now she can begin the process of embodying the goodness of the therapist inside herself. As she internalizes the caring, she feels more secure and more sure of herself. This taking in of caring from the therapist heals the hurt of the little-girl. When we say *heal*, we mean that the therapist allows the woman's previous pain and loss to be acknowledged and validated. In allowing pain, anger, and regret to emerge, the therapist and the client are transforming a deeply rooted internal experience. The therapist acknowledges the pain as legitimate: the girl wanted to be loved and accepted; this wanting, not met, was turned against the girl herself in her psyche, so that she blamed herself for not getting what she wanted. As the pain is exposed and tolerated, this formulation dissolves. The woman puts her anger and despair more outside herself and allows the therapist to come in with the love, nurturance, and attention she so badly wants. She is beginning to have a new experience of relating.

This process is not without its problems. It is often interrupted by a version of the same kind of defenses that we have seen before. The client may propose a false ending of therapy by claiming to be "cured," when the therapist sees her as just beginning to turn the corner. Or at a point when her internal object relations have begun to shift and she is embodying the love and caring of the therapist, she may become anxious. She does not need the therapist in quite the same way she did before, and she is fearful that since she is coping better, she is not entitled to continue to need and be cared for by the therapist. Some women have to be absolutely desperate before they can ask for help and be helped. If they begin to feel they can manage their lives, they expect to lose the therapist and all she is giving. The fear of loss is restimulated and they expect to be pushed away once again.

At this stage we may see one of two things. First, the woman may suggest that she is ready to end therapy. This suggestion needs to be explored in detail and at length, because it may be easy at that point, especially if the client really is feeling better in herself, for the therapist to accept the proposal at face value. Yet it is at just at this point that *why* the client feels ready to leave must be explored. There is often an unspoken sense that getting better means that one is no longer entitled to get. This is predicated on the notion that getting is the exception and only in dire circumstances is it legitimate to reach out for help in the first place.[6] The client may imagine that this is what the therapist believes and thus fear she will be pushed away. Or the relationship with the therapist may be so precious that she feels vulnerable and wants to cut herself off from it as a way of controlling the anticipated loss.

Alternatively, at this point in therapy—when the therapist feels the client is much better and the woman has acknowledged for sometime that she is feeling better in herself— suddenly the client seems to take ten steps back. She presents herself as having once more lost the ability to cope; she does not understand why this has happened, but it has happened. We have been struck by how often this response occurs and have discovered from our clients that their feeling better is problematic because part of the therapeutic work still needs to be done. It has not been made explicit between us that a woman can be feeling better and still receive nurturance and attention. Her needs for nurturance do not stop because some historic needs have been addressed. Women also have needs that are rooted in the present, and "feeling better" should not preclude the possibility that such needs can be met. At this stage the therapist should explore with the client why feeling good within herself was so frightening that she could not sustain it. She should be helped to think back a couple of weeks and remember what it was like to feel that she was coping. It is highly probable that the woman was frightened because, feeling better within herself, she imagined she would have to end the therapy. Her unconscious reaction was, "I can't cope," which is a way of saying, "I still need you, and I'm afraid that if I need you less and if I can cope, then you won't let me be here with you."

At this stage the client may use the defense of saying that she does not like the therapist, or finds her difficult or unperceptive. She may feel that the therapist does not really want to give to her at all. A client can become difficult at this point, protecting herself so carefully that she meets every move the therapist makes toward her with, "You're not doing enough"; "You're not doing it right"; "You don't really like me"; "I'm sure you don't really want to see me at five o'clock"; "I'm sure you're only forcing that smile when you see me"; "I'm sure you can't wait till the end of the session"; or alternatively, "I can't make today's appointment; my car just broke down." Sometimes the therapist has to chase the client in the sessions. The client conveys her distrust by instituting a push-pull dynamic. The therapist herself may find that within the countertransference she feels both inadequate and terribly needed.

One client, Sylvia, was a good example of these phenomena. She had been brought up by a succession of nannies and, not surprisingly, felt that women were always disappointing her and disappearing when she needed them. She would come into her therapy sessions angry and desperate and leave disgruntled and unsatisfied. She criticized the therapist constantly and considered all her interventions unhelpful. Underneath the criticism, the therapist and Sylvia were able to discern Sylvia's conviction that it was impossible for her to find a woman on whom she could rely. This conviction was in the process of being shaken by what was going on in the therapy relationship—especially the consistency of the therapist's wish to help her—and that in itself had caused some upset. It is very important for the therapist to pay special attention to a difficult period such as this, because if she is working with a woman who has been particularly deprived, she may be tempted to pull out of the relationship because of the strains on her as a therapist, and that feeling must not be communicated to the client because it will reinforce her old feelings of abandonment.

These reactions may seem paradoxical. The client wanted to feel good within herself. Why does doing so confuse and frighten her? The answer may well be that she is sure she is going to lose more than she will gain. The changes in herself, her new self-understanding and beginning self-confidence, are unfamiliar and she cannot rely on them yet. But at the same time these changes are already forcing her to change many facets of her relationships. She is exchanging the known for the unknown, a process bound to produce tension. When all these issues are discussed and worked through in the therapy, the client will feel a tremendous relief. She will finally know that feeling better and stronger can bring gains rather than loss.

The issues that a woman brings to therapy—her dependency needs, her defenses and the therapist's response to them—are the essence of the middle phase of the therapy relationship.

Ending and Separating

In the course of therapy, the client has had the chance to explore the themes of her inner life in a new way. She has encountered a particular kind of support for exploring personal issues and encouragement to clarify what is important, conflictual, and painful for her. Her real-life situation may have changed and certainly her perception of herself will not be the same. At the same time another process has occurred: the client has experienced the nurturing of the therapist. In the context of a genuine relationship between two women, the client can take in and embody the nurturing aspects of the therapist.

These experiences promote a feeling of well-being and provide for more integration of the ego. As the woman's internal world changes, she comes to be more self-accepting, and less of her is hidden away. In turn she is now able to experience feeling loved, and to experience herself as being lovable. She feels entitled to nurturance, entitled to contact, worthy of good things and of living her own life. Learning to feel that the little-girl inside is accepted, understood, and loved by the therapist is an extremely important part of the healing process.[7]

Throughout the process of therapy the woman is experimenting with ways of showing who she is, of bringing her little-girl self, her needs, and her vulnerabilities into safe relationships in the world outside therapy. What the therapist sees, and what the client is experiencing for herself, is a reduction in the discrepancy between the part of her that comes into therapy and the part that is out in the world. The therapist has encouraged the woman to bring her little-girl needs into the therapy relationship and also into other relationships with friends and with lovers. This interaction in other social relationships helps to integrate the little-girl part into the whole person. So, for example, Anne finally was able to ask her husband to pay attention to her when she told him about something that concerned her. She was able to feel justified in wanting him to listen carefully and seriously. The woman brings back her experiences outside therapy for discussion with the therapist, and together they explore the woman's feelings of being more whole and complete in the outside world.

As the little-girl is accepted and integrated by the woman and by her therapist, friends, and lovers, she finds herself being listened to and nurtured. She has experience with showing her needs, and this in itself is a major step forward whether or not they are responded to. She has a sense that exposing her needs is not a disaster. She develops a confidence that in listening to her own inner voices she is in touch with an authentic self and this increases her ability to pursue what she wants. She feels more whole so that even disappointments or rejections do not signify utter disintegration. She feels a strength in herself which she could not rely on before. She no longer feels herself to be a screaming mass of unending needs. She feels less insatiable, less needy. She is also less judgmental of herself, less anxious, and less critical. Trusting that she knows herself better, she can relate more directly, with a reasonable expectation that her needs and her identity will be taken into account by others.

Therapist and client together have been building the woman's sense of self. Now this new and reasonably secure sense of self provides for a continuity of experience at an internal level. The woman reflects her own sense of being secure within herself and meets situations and relationships with this new substantive feeling. She is no longer the person she imagined others wanted her to be. She no longer compulsively adapts her personality to fit the needs of others in order to feel accepted.

The feeding, acceptance, and transformation of the little-girl changes the woman's internal object relations. This change at the psychic structural level brings changes in the woman's dependency needs. These needs change because they have been met over and over again in the course of therapy. The continued meeting of needs means that she can feel connection without merger. She has a sense of her own boundaries. She does not need her therapist, her lover, her children, her friends in precisely the same way. She does not depend on connections with them in order to have a self, nor acquire her sense of self through them. She has a self.

Her little-girl part has had a chance to be engaged with and thus integrated, and she can now relate as a whole person, who like all human beings is dependent on and interdependent with others. This is very important because the goal of therapy is not in any sense to avoid being dependent on people. To be autonomous, to have a sense of self, to feel nurtured, to feel less insatiable, does not mean that one does not have needs. What it does mean is that the basis of the needs has shifted, and that opens up the possibility that they can actually be met. It is often this internal sense of well-being that allows people to enter intimate relationships. When Sylvia felt less desperate in her need for a man to define her life, she was actually able to begin a fulfilling relationship with James. She felt she had something to give, and she was able to look at him as a separate person whom she enjoyed.

At the point in therapy when a woman begins to feel that she no longer needs her therapist in the same way and begins to experience a change in herself in relation to the therapy, therapy may no longer make sense in the same way it did before. The client is experiencing herself in other relationships outside therapy and enjoying what she experiences. She feels her autonomy. She may now begin to suggest to the therapist, in all sorts of different ways, the idea of separating from her and ending the therapy.

In contrast to the premature moves toward separation that are likely to occur in the middle stage of therapy, this initiative by the client will not seem hasty. Most likely both therapist and client will be thinking of separation at somewhat the same time—within a period of perhaps three months. The separation process has its own themes that need to be worked through; they will take time and require the same attention to detail that characterizes all phases of the therapy relationship. The client may be hesitant about bringing up the idea of leaving and extremely tentative when she first broaches the subject. She may be afraid the therapist will not support her autonomy and her strength and may fear her disapproval. In addition, the client may imagine that she is stirring up feelings of competition and envy in the therapist, who will then in some way try to hold her back. She may anticipate that somehow her good feelings about herself will threaten the therapist.

The starting point for working on these feelings is that women, because of the ambivalences in the mother-daughter relationship, have not had the experience of feeling their strength and separateness supported. Women often share and feel equal and close in their distress and lack of confidence, but many women find it strange and difficult to feel equal with each other in their strengths without having allied feelings of competition and envy. When Joyce's best friend, Elaine, got accepted to law school, Joyce felt excited for her but at the same time was flooded with feelings of upset and envy. In analyzing these uncomfortable feelings we learned that Elaine's success brought up feelings of insecurity, unentitlement, and abandonment for Joyce. Somehow she felt that similar successes or accomplishments would not be possible for both of them and that she would be left behind. These kind of feelings will need to be worked through over and over again in the last phase of the therapy relationship. The client needs repeated experiences of being supported in her strength. She needs to feel that her successes and her autonomy are truly appreciated and that the therapist's support is not a one-time fluke.

Women feel tentative about separation based on growth because it is such a new experience. It is not part of a little girl's development to be actively supported for being separate. The mother-daughter push-pull leaves memories of danger and confusion around separation. In therapy there is an opportunity to practice being autonomous until it feels all right, just as the toddler once practiced walking until that felt safe. The woman's expectations of disapproval, envy, or competition are defenses against her potential independence. It is extremely important for the therapist to help the client bring up such fears and to explore the woman's wishes for separation in great detail.

At the beginning of the therapy relationship there was an inequality of vulnerability and neediness. In the course of therapy this power relationship has shifted and the woman, through her integration of the little-girl, now feels herself an adult, more nearly an equal of her therapist. Now she is exploring yet another level of acceptance and struggling to feel this new kind of support. She needs to take in her therapist's acceptance of her new way of being.

A different kind of fear that a woman may have when she brings up the idea of ending therapy is that somehow she is rejecting the therapist and making her feel inadequate. She feels as if she is saying, "I'm rejecting what you still have to give me, I don't need that any more," and that this belittles or diminishes what the therapist has given. In her anxiety about upsetting the therapist she may want to reassure her that she still needs her. We have discussed this dynamic in the mother-daughter relationship, in which the daughter's attempts at separation make her anxious and is difficult for the mother as well, because as the daughter tries to separate from mother, mother fears the loss of her sense of self. In this phase of the therapy relationship we may find the client caught up in trying to reassure the therapist that she is not going to be abandoned. Women often do this by presenting the therapist with new problems to be worked on, but this in itself is an issue to be looked at in the therapy. In our experience it is often an expression of the client's difficulty in accepting the therapist's support and approval of her wish for separation.

Another issue that frequently emerges during the separation process centers on the woman's gradual awareness of the differences between herself and her therapist. As she increasingly experiences her therapist as a separate person, not merely as a provider to her, the client gradually begins to experience more of the therapist's personality and opinions. Her internal object relations have changed, and she now has true boundaries and the confidence that enables her to feel that she and her therapist can work together toward understanding without the requirement that they be always in unison. The therapist has provided an experience of being in unison with the client, and this has given her security. The knowledge of being understood opens the way for the client to notice her differences from the therapist. Views her therapist expresses which at an earlier time were distressing or threatening now take on a new significance. The separateness which these differing views symbolize can be tolerated because the woman is both in relationship with and separate from her therapist.

An important part of the separation process in feminist therapy is to make sure the client does not feel that separation from the therapist will mean that she must contain and cope with all her needs on her own, that she cannot bring her needs to others. This is why we have come to believe that it is important for the therapist to remain available as a therapist after the therapy has ended. Even though the woman has embodied the therapist, and the experiences of their relationship will thus live on inside her, it is nevertheless vital for her to feel that the therapist continues to be someone she can reach out to if the need arises.[8] We consider it important for a woman to be able to leave therapy without feeling any repetition of her earlier sense of being pushed away from maternal nurturance. Separating from a feminist therapist should not mean that when the client no longer needs her therapist in the same way, she loses her permanently.

The ability to be autonomous does not mean that the client no longer needs love and support. One of our clients when ending her therapy said, "Somehow it feels like a love affair, a good love affair that's ending—and that doesn't make sense because you don't leave a love affair that's working very well." Feminist therapy is about learning to love the little-girl inside that patriarchy has taught us to fear and despise; it is about allowing her to grow up and become part of an autonomous woman; above all, it is about being loved by another woman and helped by her to grow and become separate.

This process of therapy and the model we have been describing, then, are informed by the theoretical understanding of women's psychological development as outlined in chapter 2. This theory suggests new ways of understanding the content, the transference, and the real relationship between the two people engaged in therapy together. This new understanding provides the beginnings of a theory about the practice of a feminist psychoanalysis.

Notes

1. See Luise Eichenbaum and Susie Orbach, *What Do Women Want? Exploding the Myth of Dependency,* New York, 1983.

2. It is focusing on these aspects of a woman's psychology and how they occur within the therapy relationship that makes it especially feminist. The therapist is not pushing these feelings away but has the confidence that she can cope with the upset and the longing. In supervising the work of other therapists we have often noticed how the therapist subtly or not so subtly indicates her discomfort with such feelings to the client, thus unwittingly reproducing aspects of the maternal push-pull dynamic. We think this occurs because centrality of gender and feminine socialization have been overlooked and unknowingly the therapist, possibly still wary of her own dependency needs, feels negative about those of the client.

3. We have noticed that many therapists feel so frustrated by these tests that they unintentionally extend their life by interpreting them as a defense. At this point in therapy the client may experience this attitude as a pushing away and thus a confirmation that she cannot trust the therapist. In other words, the defense works too well. It achieves its aim of pushing the therapist away.

4. See Dorothy Dinnerstein, *The Mermaid and the Minotaur: Sexual Arrangements and Human Malaise,* New York, 1976.

5. D. W. Winnicott writes, "My thesis is that what we do in therapy is to attempt to imitate the natural process that characterises the behaviour of any mother with her own infant. It is the mother-infant couple that can teach us the basic principles on which we may base our therapeutic work."

6. This is an injunction that works in gender-linked ways. Men may be loath to seek help because of the stigma attached to showing vulnerability. However, their needs for nurturance are often addressed in unacknowledged ways. Women, on the other hand, often seek help, and in fact exhibit a learned helplessness, but help is usually affirmed in the form of getting them back on their feet to function—that is, to look after others—until the next collapse. Our approach posits that a woman can be feeling better within herself and still be entitled to get.

7. Although these goals and achievements are not unique to a feminist psychotherapy, classical therapy does not always apply them specifically to women. Such feelings in women fly in the face of the rules of patriarchy. In this sense, then, the goal is informed by feminist protest and feminist vision.

8. Obviously this ideal is not always achievable: therapists move from agency to agency or city to city. In general we believe that even under these circumstances, when the therapy has ended appropriately the therapist should be available in some capacity, perhaps prepared to reply to the occasional letter. When the client's therapy was not finished and she transferred to another therapist, contact is obviously more problematic. Generally speaking, we do not think that changing the therapy relationship into some other kind of relationship, a friendship for example, is useful.

CHAPTER 5

Women's Theme-Centered Workshops and Psychodynamic Therapy Groups

Theme-Centered Workshops

At The Women's Therapy Centre in London we have led a variety of theme-centered groups working on topics that emerged in individual therapy sessions, in our staff supervision, and in study groups. Some of the women who participate in these groups are themselves self-consciously feminist, while at least half the participants do not see themselves in that way. The heterogeneous nature of the women involved notwithstanding, the issues that have come up have resonated at a psychological level for all of them—young or old, married or single, working outside the home or not. This is a dramatic confirmation that women's experience, though individually felt and structurally isolated, is socially similar.

The topics themselves range from dependency, competition, sexuality, mothers and daughters, anger, and jealousy to issues around power, difficulties in intimate relationships, giving and receiving, compulsive eating, and anorexia (see chapter 7 for specific discussion of some of these themes). In addition, colleagues have held workshops on such subjects as guilt, aging, fathers and daughters, mothers and children, and body image.[1] In all these workshops the emphasis has been on exploring painful and complicated themes with a view to increasing understanding of the underlying dynamics in each woman's individual psychology as well as opening up space for a new relationship to the issue to emerge.

The group workshops are structured differently from the individual therapy session, perhaps with an initial exposition by the workshop leader on why this particular topic is a problem area for women; a round-the-room session in which participants share their reasons for coming; and then an exercise—often a guided fantasy—designed to uncover the relationship each woman has to the subject.[2] The group continues with individual work with the participants, general discussion, role play, and homework designed to help each woman think through a new position to the problem theme. The workshops, then, are designed not simply to open up issues but to provide new solutions.

Much of what we have learned about women's psychology in the workshop setting has confirmed what we see in our individual sessions. Neither experience substitutes for the other: workshop groups and individual sessions serve different purposes. Because in a theoretical sense the two kinds of work dovetail, here we want to point out the value of these workshops.

Being in a group with other women may be a novel experience in itself. Many women have never spent intentional time together, time in which they can both reflect on and be active in relation to their experience. Much of women's time is, of course, spent with other women, but in contexts that women have not necessarily chosen themselves and that therefore do not have the same meaning.[3] Because of this self-determined coming together, the women in the group are with other women in a new way. As they make contact with each other and work together at a psychological level, the process of valuing each other and themselves starts. Women are, in a myriad of both overt and subtle ways, discouraged from taking themselves or their experiences seriously. Now, sharing them in the workshop, women are in fact taking each other's experiences seriously. In turn this attitude is reflected back to each woman in the room, for as she notices the contribution others make, she can begin to conceive that her presence, her opening up aspects of herself, and her interventions are of value. The insights that come out of such workshops are especially significant, because they are born of women sharing and exploring together, revealing intimate aspects of their internal experiences, and discovering how much they have in common beneath the surface.

This new way of coming together is an important step in breaking out of one's isolation. Sharing in a safe environment aspects of one's experience in itself helps ease the psychic distress caused by isolation in the home and in individual relationships. The new experience breaks an old pattern.[4] It is a challenge and opens doors to further exploration and possibilities. Twelve women sitting together focusing on a theme in their lives is a dramatic, tender, upsetting, and inspiring experience. Many workshops have a certain electricity, as the women painfully build together a psychological picture of their lives.

Because of their psychosocial development women tend to be attentive, supportive, and "appropriate good givers." The positive aspects of this giving can create a nurturing group in which women take in caring from other women. Coming to a group may be nerve-racking at first, for one may feel trepidation about what will be uncovered and other participants' issues may spark unanticipated exposures, but precisely because of women's capacity to give,[5] there is often an atmosphere of tremendous caring and concern, which creates a safe climate for exploration of issues in each individual's psychology.

Related to their psychological skill of giving is women's ability to tune in to others, to pick up the nuances and significance of others' experience. This helps a woman imagine what another woman is feeling as she tells her story. For a woman to be immediately understood by other women in the group is tremendously reassuring. Such understanding should not in any way curtail her from exploring, articulating, and expressing the parts that others do not understand, but when she says, "My husband was talking to a woman at a party for a long time and I felt I shouldn't be jealous, there was nothing really to be jealous of, but I did feel jealous," she gets an immediate and empathetic understanding which allows the other women to explore with her, for her and themselves, why that was such an uncomfortable situation. She does not have to explain that it was upsetting—they all understand and know from their own feelings that it was.

Two other factors make workshops extremely productive settings. The very fact of a workshop centered on something a woman has experienced in her own life (and something she would like help with) reduces the shame and embarrassment that attaches to such feelings as competition, jealousy, envy, and anger. The possibility of looking at such feelings makes them less threatening. In addition, because the participants do not necessarily have close relationships with each other and the meeting time is limited, the transference manifestations which are so much a part of the therapeutic relationship are reduced. There is sensitivity to and support for each woman's struggle with the particular theme. Participants do not need to make a long-term commitment to such a group to gain enormously from it.

Women's Psychodynamic Therapy Groups

Psychodynamic therapy groups, unlike workshops, focus on interactions among participants and on the dynamics of the group process. In our discussion of individual therapy in chapters 3 and 4 we saw that the relationship between therapist and client is critical, and this is also true of therapy groups. Usually each woman joining this kind of group makes a commitment to it for an open-ended period of time, though some psychodynamic groups specify the life of the group as perhaps a year. Unlike a workshop, which one can often join without a prior meeting with the group leader, an ongoing psychodynamic group involves an "intake session" with the psychotherapist for an assessment of whether the group is appropriate for the client.

The psychodynamics in an all-women therapy group are different from those in a mixed-sex group. A feminist therapist working in either an all-women or a mixed group will draw out dynamics within the group and make interpretations about individuals' needs and feelings within a framework that differs from other analytic groups.[6] Observations about mothers and daughters, daughters and fathers, and feelings of envy, competition, inadequacy, and longing take on new meaning. But in an all-women therapy group the therapist is always struck by the vast amount of need. From the first meeting onward, this need is a critical dynamic from which many other dynamics spring.

We have discovered that, when a therapy group begins, many silences and difficulties in using the time there is, or too many references to other situations in which the woman has felt unsatisfied, frustrated, misunderstood, or cut short means that each woman feels enormous anxiety about there not being "enough." The therapist generally interprets these worries as expressions of an underlying anxiety about whether the group can be a safe, dependable place for participants to bring their needs and be understood.

Just as in the workshops, each group member is acutely aware of the needs of the other women in the group. Thus we encounter a second major dynamic, and this one traps the group member in conflict. How can she take space and get help within the group when there is so much need around her? How can she take the time she needs without feeling that she has taken too much? She will feel guilty for receiving attention and nurturance and feels that this "getting" on her part "took away" from the other women; frightened that her floodgates have begun to open and her feelings may now overwhelm her (and perhaps the group); worried that the other group members will be angry with her for being so greedy or envious of her for having the attention and care of the therapist.

As a result of these conflicts, specific dynamics emerge in relation to the therapist. Her very presence exposes the neediness that exists in the room at the same time that it provides safety for its exposure. As we have seen in other situations, women try to hide their neediness, their little-girl inside, but being in a therapy group is itself a step toward vulnerability, a statement that one does have needs. Women in the group may cope with the internal tensions produced by the presence of the therapist (a potential nurturer and satisfier) by trying to keep her out. The group may form a tentative alliance, putting the therapist just outside. Her interventions and interpretations may be met with caution and fear, as each woman and then the group as a whole tries to contain the need, so that the group itself reproduces the false boundaries between the needs and the group.

The therapist represents a breaker of these false boundaries as well as a potential nurturer. The group holds the hope of each member that it will be a place where help can be got, where isolation can be broken down and pain released and tolerated. But the group often defends itself against these hopes and against potential disappointment by the therapist. Each member unconsciously feels that the therapist will not be able to handle all the emotions here, that she, another woman, will not be strong enough to contain the group. As a result we see many dynamics developed to keep the therapist at bay, as defenses against this potential disappointment.

In the therapy group, just as in individual therapy, there are both real relationships and transference relationships. Mother-daughter transference onto the therapist as well as among group members is abundant. Many exchanges in the group trigger transference feelings and ensuing feelings of anger, disappointment, or being misunderstood. Indeed, transference in a group is more obvious than in individual therapy, because every woman here has transferential feelings both toward the therapist and toward group members. The therapist both observes this and experiences the transference in strikingly clear ways.

As the group relaxes more and there are fewer defenses against wanting from the therapist, there may be struggles for her attention. When she gives attention to one woman it may trigger the other members' own longings, feelings of loss or not getting enough, fears of instability, and competitive feelings toward other women. At the same time they may feel relief as they see the therapist's ability to handle and help another group member: perhaps she can be there for them too.

Because of the transference feelings and all the other feelings each woman brings into a therapy group, there are times when she feels surrounded by her feelings and perhaps encapsulated, isolated, within them. She wants contact with the other group members, but this is not easy or straightforward. There are so many feelings filling the room—so much potential merger, boundarylessness, and loss of self—that the transference seems to be bouncing off the circle the women have created. These feelings are so central to women that one can feel surrounded by generations of their history and social experience. Women talk of their mothers, grandmothers, sisters, and of the effects all these have had. Feelings one woman may express of vulnerability, pain, or anger are identified with by other group members.

At times the feelings that flood in seem so overwhelming that there are attempts to subdue them. Group members may cut off a woman who is expressing her pain because of their own feelings of pain and their identification with the woman who is "working." The interruption is an attempt to quash the feelings, to repress them in the same way she does her own similar feelings. A group member's "inability" to understand or tendency to be perplexed at or dismissive of another's experiences is also a defense against her own similar feelings. This dynamic parallels aspects of the mother-daughter relationship, in which mother pushes away aspects of her daughter's personality because the daughter's expression of certain needs and feelings stirs up similar ones that the mother herself must contain.

Another attempt at repression and containment is the

phenomenon of subgrouping. Fear of exposure and a desire to cover up lead some women to hold on to one or several other members of the group. Anxieties about the group's open-endedness and the lack of boundaries that symbolizes, along with fear of being out of control, create a dynamic of subgrouping in the hope of containment and security. Subgroupings provide interesting work for the group at two levels. In understanding and interpreting this dynamic, the therapist provides a different form of containment and security that allows group members to work on the second product of these subgroupings: the feelings of exclusion or inclusion of those outside or inside each subgroup, whether or not they are in another subgroup. These subgroupings are best understood as attempts to grab onto a sense of self, just as adolescents experience their peer group as essential to the development of an identity. A woman as an individual within the group may feel too insecure, too insubstantial to stand by herself; as so often before, she seeks identity through her connection to others. Thus these feelings of inclusion-exclusion open up the woman's past experiences of inclusion and exclusion in the family, at school, or at work. Triangles of all sorts—mother, father, client; sister, mother, client—emerge, and with them come rich material to be worked on in the group.

As women work on such issues within the group, another dynamic flows through the process. In a group where there are perhaps eight women there will be eight "little-girls," and finding out that every woman has a little-girl aspect is extremely reassuring. This discovery also makes each woman's own little-girl self less frightening to her. This, of course, is therapeutic in itself, but, perhaps more significant, as the women are able to be more sympathetic to other women's little-girls inside and the dilemma that other women feel about this part of themselves they become sympathetic to their own little-girl selves. Jean was able to see how group member Carol, whom she respected for being self-assured, outgoing, and professionally competent, judged and criticized herself for any expression of uncertainty. Jean felt stunned by how brutal and uncharitable Carol could be toward herself. She pointed this out to her patiently and eventually Carol was able to ease up on herself and accept that she could be vulnerable and unknowing. She didn't collapse under the acceptance of these aspects of her personality; in fact, it showed a kind of strength that Jean could in turn draw on in her struggle to be more self-accepting.

As each woman experiences receiving from both the other group members and the therapist, she becomes able to express her resentments, her upsets, her fears of abandonment. And the therapist, precisely because she is making herself available within a therapeutic context, can work through these issues and help the woman experience taking in all this caring. Being in an all-women therapy group and having a therapist who is able to handle and provide nurturance to several needy little-girls is a very positive experience.

Another theme that is woven into the group is that all women want validation and they want it from women. Perhaps the most difficult thing for a mother to give her daughter is a sense of self-worth, because she identifies with her daughter and lacks a sense of her own self-worth. For that reason women come to seek validation from their fathers and then from other men. But our practice suggests that the search for validation relates to difficulties in the mother-daughter relationship and that what women really want is validation from other women. In a women's therapy group a woman has a chance to redirect her search or validation through her relationships with other women.

118

As women begin to see each other as multidimensional—to move away from that deeply held picture of woman as good or bad, needy or insatiable, all-powerful or all-withholding—they can begin to apply that multidimensional texture to their own experience of themselves. As they listen to other women they begin to take each woman's experiences seriously and thereby to take their own the same way. Thus they begin to reverse deeply internalized feelings of low self-worth.

The experience of a women's therapy group is exciting, fascinating, deeply painful, and often radically transforming. One of the central dynamics in the group process is that the women develop a trust in the continuity of the group. The women's early anxiety about "will there be enough" and their unconscious preparation for loss, their desperation about trying to get their needs out and met in a limited time, will change dramatically as they begin to trust the continuity of the group and to feel that its nurturance and support is available for them as long as they need it.

Women in the group, then, work through a process of acceptance, discharge of pain, anger, upset, and an understanding of unconscious patterns and psychological life. And as her needs change, each woman moves toward the process of separation from the group. Thus, a critical issue at a later stage of the analytic women's therapy group is that of separation and autonomy. The therapist and the other group members help each woman reverse the earlier experience of incomplete separation from mother and to move forward with other strong, separate, nurtured, loving women, still connected in healthy contact. As in individual therapy, this is a delicate process. In the group, one woman's proposed departure may spark other members' feelings of abandonment or anger. The departure of any member, whether premature or appropriate, produces a rich situation for all involved, especially when the therapist is working to help each woman experience a sense of autonomy and separateness.

Notes

1. There are about twelve workshops a week and their average total attendance is a hundred women.

2. Some of the groups at The Women's Therapy Centre are designed to become leaderless self-help groups and are structured along those lines. See Sheila Ernst and Lucy Goodison, *In Our Own Hands,* London, 1981.

3. In a factory there may be only women on an assembly line, but this structure is created by managers, who tend to be men. In the house a woman may spend time with women friends, but that does not make it a woman-only environment; it is often a relegation.

4. The form of the women's group evolves, of course, from the women's liberation movement, where women first sought out other women and met in consciousness-raising or "rap" groups as a way to understand their individual and isolated experience.

5. See Jean Baker Miller, *Toward a New Psychology of Women,* Boston, Mass., 1976, for a discussion of such positive aspects of women's experience that are deeply a part of each woman's psychology.

6. In a women-only therapy group, because women are not having to compete with or against men, the feelings of being second-class, of being invalid within a group, have less opportunity to be reinforced. A single-sex group makes for very different power dynamics. The introduction of a man into a group of women breaks and changes this dynamic.

A mixed therapy group run by a feminist therapist will be aware of the meaning of gender in the group dynamics. With a feminist perspective one is aware of the sexual politics of the group; how the presence of women and men affects each of the sexes; how women relate to men; how women relate to women when men are present; how men relate to women; and, of course, how men relate to each other when women are present. One is also aware that the women may select different material in a mixed therapy group and a women's therapy group. Many observations could be made about a feminist perspective on mixed groups, but this is not the subject here. Let us just focus on three issues to look at in leading a mixed group.

First, what happens when a man actually opens up in the therapy group? Who is attentive to him, who nurtures him? Is it the women, is it the men? Do the men feel inadequate at nurturing, and are the women, therefore, taking on the nurturing role, or is that challenged within the group? Similarly, how do men cope with women's upset and neediness in the group? Do they run away from it and leave other women to cope with it, or do they struggle with their own fears and inadequacies?

Second, how is competition manifested between the women and the men and between the men and the men? This is a very interesting aspect of sexual politics to look at.

Third, in addition, of course, you get a tremendous amount of anger stirring: men's anger with women for being so powerful and so withholding and with all the images of womanhood and women's sexuality; and, of course, women's anger and women's placatory stance toward men.

A feminist therapist can be very helpful in pinpointing these dynamics in a mixed-therapy group.

In our postgraduate training workshops at The Women's Therapy Centre, we look at the following questions:

(a) Who takes space in the group (issues related to this)?

(b) Who takes care of whom in mixed therapy groups?

(c) How do women and men relate differentially to women and men therapists?

(d) How are issues around women's autonomy or connectedness experienced by group members and how are they interpreted by the therapist?

(e) Is there anxiety in the group related to women's separateness?

(f) How is female/male sexuality worked on in groups?

(g) Are issues around vulnerability more difficult for men? Do they feel they must maintain an image? How do men's defenses differ from women's, and how do they serve them?

(h) What do women in group feel about men's vulnerability or feelings of inadequacy?

(i) How does a feminist analysis of the family and power relations based on sexual lines affect interpretations of group dynamics?

(j) How does a feminist analysis of the family affect transference interpretations in relation to both the therapist and other group members?

CHAPTER 6

Issues for
the Psychotherapist

THE analysis that therapists use to understand the lives and psychic conflicts of our clients applies equally well to ourselves as therapists. As women with feminist consciousness working with women we are aware of the similarities between our own and our client's lives. We may observe dynamics in the transferential aspects of the therapy relationship which are reminiscent of our own daughter-mother, mother-daughter relationship. Although this could be interpreted as countertransference material,[1] such a view seems to us rather limited. Women therapists were all girls who were taught to be women; we all have little-girls inside us; we all share on some level the same struggle for self-actualization; we all feel anger at the individual and social position of women. As women who have shared the same socialization process, we inevitably find many points of identification with our clients and identify strongly with them. This is far more than countertransference; it is the attitude and stance we purposely adopt toward hearing our own lives spread out before us by our clients, and it is what makes this kind of therapy work. To scrutinize our emotional responses to our clients requires a particular sensitivity on the part of feminist psychotherapists, who must distinguish among countertransference responses—that is, the response to the client's transferences (countertransference is the necessary complement of transference[2]), the empathy the client engenders in the therapist, the therapist's identification, and the therapist's own transference issues.

Feminist therapy acknowledges the material and structural basis of the distress of individual women and recognizes that the psychological development of female therapists has not been substantially different from that of their women clients. For this reason clinical meetings and supervision groups[3] in which therapists can think through their reactions to their clients provide needed support for the therapist and are an important part of training. In addition, we prescribe for ourselves as therapists the same method we sought as women trying to break our isolation—consciousness-raising groups for practicing therapists. These groups encourage therapists to discuss issues in which they identify with their women clients.

Such identification is one of the burdens of being a therapist. We listen again and again to the stories of our lives— lives of oppression, compromise, disappointment, frustration, unexpressed rage, and staggering bravery. We see again and again how much of this pain stems from the sexual arrangements within patriarchy, distilled through the individual nuclear family. As therapists we need a place to let off steam, to clarify our own emotional reactions, work out the connections between the emotional issues that confront us and the underlying social issues, and see how all of these relate to psychological phenomena and the work of therapy. Ideally, the supervision setting integrates these dimensions.

We do not find it of therapeutic value to share these identifications with clients, except perhaps in the most general way in the initial stages of deciding to work together. There are several reasons why we do not think it serves a positive function to disclose our own experiences to our clients. First, it becomes a burden to the client to care *for* the therapist, be concerned *for* the therapist, rather than examining the difficulties of her being in therapy *for herself.* Here too a woman's need and ability to be responsive to others can act as a great inhibitor to self-actualization. The therapy context is the place to explore this dynamic (with a view to changing it), not to reinforce it. Second, revelations of the therapist's personal experiences may serve to short-circuit what is in the client's mind, again distracting her from her own experiences. Concentrating on one's own experience takes practice. Women frequently feel guilty at talking and thinking about themselves in this way, but therapy should provide just such a place away from the client's need to respond to others. If we therapists talk about ourselves, we are in effect giving a double message to the woman in therapy: This is a safe place to talk about yourself, but only if you take account of me.

A third reason for not sharing our identification directly is that, although we provide a model for autonomy, we do not wish to encourage our clients to overidentify with us, so that they then have yet another struggle to free themselves from the imitation of a new authority figure. This is not a trivial point. During certain phases in the therapy—especially in entering the middle stage, when the client is embodying the nurturance of the therapist—the client may model aspects of herself on the therapist. This kind of modeling dissipates as the therapy proceeds and the client has the confidence to discover who she herself is and what she likes. This is part of the process of individuation, which comes after a satisfactory bonding with the therapist. A fourth reason is that self-disclosure by the therapist would cut off and interrupt the transference projections that are an essential aspect of the therapy relationship and process. It is difficult to untangle the client's projections if she is overloaded with real information about the therapist that is extraneous to the therapy.

Often a client will wish that the therapist would share more of her own life and personal experience. Because women's lives are structurally isolated, hearing of each other's experiences can be enormously supportive. If the client is especially isolated, she may feel odd or peculiar, and even if she feels understood by the therapist she may also need other affirmation and sharing. The therapist may be tempted to gratify this desire, but we have found it better for the therapist to examine the client's feelings directly. In addition the therapist may help her client to bring up such issues with women friends or to join a group in which experiences can be shared: a group-therapy setting, a theme workshop, or, of course, a consciousness-raising group.

So in a sense the therapist herself must hold back in a particular way. But this does not mean that she is witholding. While she restrains her impulse to show the client by personal examples that her confusions, questions, and concerns are not unique, she finds other ways to reassure her. The feeling that one is odd—unlike others in a negative way—occurs frequently because of the social and psychological requirement that women should live in an outer-directed way, focusing their attention on others. Turning inward and tracing one's own authentic experiences may well bring up feelings, sensations, and ideas that are not only unfamiliar but at odds with one's self-conception. The therapist can help the client with such initial concerns by reminding herself of her own first therapy appointment and the vulnerability, hope, fear, and other feelings that accompanied it.

When a therapist undertakes therapy with a woman client she opens herself up to a serious new relationship that will encompass intimacy and tenderness on both sides as the therapy proceeds. The therapy relationship not only affects the client but has deep meaning in the therapist's life. Both women are working together to try to understand the client's emotional distress. The therapist, outside the client's actual confusing or tortured experience, is an emotional buoy, supporting the client in her struggle to come through the repeating patterns of stress. The therapist must be able to view what the client is sharing with her from a nonjudgmental position, because a significant early part of the curative process is to help clients break through the shame that accompanies their thoughts, feelings, fantasies, and desires, as a prelude to working through the difficult themes that lie beneath the inhibition. This therapeutic role is immensely rewarding, but it carries its own difficulties.

Separate from identification and empathy, and the fact that not sharing can sometimes be more difficult for the therapist than sharing, is the issue of the therapist's transference. The client will inevitably trigger in the therapist conflicts in her own life. These may be current conflicts or buried issues from the past. Unless the therapist is sufficiently aware of these conflicts, and of her attitudes, prejudices, and blind spots, she may, without realizing it, try to use the therapy to satisfy inappropriate needs. To reduce the possibility of acting on their own unconscious processes, all therapists go through intensive psychotherapy themselves. This training analysis is the first protection against abuse. It should insure that the psychotherapist can distinguish between her needs and the client's needs and be unambiguously available to the client within the therapy setting. But since no training analysis can claim to have exposed every nook and cranny of the psyche, or to have worked through every troublesome issue in the therapist's life, it is important for her to be alert to the feelings that the client arouses and to distinguish where they come from. Are they a response to the client's transference—for example, an expression of role responsiveness?[4] Or are they a trigger to the therapist's personal, unresolved issue?

Without constant monitoring of her own feeling and awareness of the possibility of countertransference, the therapist may offer interpretations or areas for exploration that have more meaning for her than for the client. For example, the therapist in a women's therapy group is exposed to a tremendous amount of upset, distress, need, boundarylessness, self-hate, anger, and competition, as well as love and nurturing. She must be able to tolerate all of this with confidence. She must transmit to the group, through her behavior and relatedness, the knowledge that she will not be overwhelmed or annihilated by the group. She may at times, especially toward the beginning of the group, fear that there is so much need she cannot possibly meet it. At times she will feel pushed out of the group, and she must be able to tolerate the rejection, anger, criticism, and negative transference that both individual members and the group as a whole direct toward her. She must be acutely aware of the underlying emotions the women are expressing, because so much that occurs on the surface is only a clue to what the real emotional and therapeutic issues are. Above all, the therapist must be keenly aware of her own boundaries. There is so much merger and boundarylessness in the group that she will at times feel swamped and taken over by all the feelings, needs, and little-girls in the group. She must be able to remain separate and in her own boundaries if she is to interpret for the group, work with all its members, and be a safe and stable figure for them.

During the course of therapy the therapist becomes extremely important in the client's life. She becomes a reference point, a consistent figure who holds and contains the client and is available with outstretched hand to work through any and all emotional troubles. When the client feels discouraged or despairing the therapist does not collapse with her but is a stable force. She helps to frame the psychic distress and in so doing points to new possibilities. The client has come to the therapist with needs, with hopes for help, and with her notions, conscious and unconscious, about what is possible in relationships.

The therapist is seen as powerful because she aids the client, and this dependency has its allied feelings of powerlessness and helplessness. We have seen how in the transference aspect of the therapeutic relationship the feelings and attitudes learned in infancy from the caregiver come up for examination. But these are also of concern outside the scope of the transference, because the client is not merely imagining that she is more vulnerable and less powerful than the therapist. There is a real power differential in this relationship. The contract in therapy is that, first, both client and therapist are committed to using the energy and skills at hand to understand and work through the psychic distress of the client. At various stages of the therapy the client will feel her need for the therapist more or less acutely. The therapist does not have a parallel need for the client, however much she may enjoy working with a particular woman. The therapist's confidence about the task that confronts her means that she is bringing a different part of herself to the therapy situation from the client: she does not show her vulnerability. Although there are many other ways in which this power differential is manifested, one of the most important is that the therapist makes the interpretations and maintains the overview of the client's psyche. Both people recognize this aspect of her knowledge, and both are aware that this way of knowing is a kind of power.

The client will have a range of feelings about the power differential, and it is important for the therapist to be clear about this dynamic so that she can help the client explore her quite understandable fears and anxieties about potential abuse within this setting. The therapist should not deny the power she has, but observe its impact in each particular therapy relationship. The general social requirement that women defer to others may propel a woman to defer in her therapy, and it may not occur to her that there is anything amiss in doing so. Other women may respond differently. Aware of having been tampered with by authority figures, a client may express caution and concern about what could be "done to me" in the therapy. Such concerns should be taken seriously and compassionately by the therapist because they are often rooted in real experiences of abuse.

Worries about the power differential will find their place for discussion at various stages within the therapy, and it will be important to sort through with the client the various levels and meanings of her feelings of vulnerability. At times it may be important to validate that her vulnerability is real and that the therapist and client are in different positions within the relationship.

One way of minimizing the power differential is to demystify aspects of the therapy relationship. As the client is able to understand the background of her confusing emotional states, she will become aware of her own voice and strength. She can share the language of psychological affairs and understand its meaning. There is no need for a therapist to withhold information about what she understands of the client's psychic processes if the knowledge will give the woman more perspective on and understanding of herself and the therapy process.

The therapist should be open to talking about her theoretical biases, her prejudices, and how her theory and practice view the psychology of women. The client is entitled to know what sort of therapy she is committing herself to. Ideas about the psyche are thought about in particular ways, which means simply that all *therapies are informed by a political perspective.* Psychotherapists often make the mistake of offering up their clinical work as though it were value-free. In this sense they are unconscious of how a political view of the world shapes a psychological view of women and how this in turn provides a particular viewpoint. As feminist psychotherapists we consciously bring our political and personal attitudes, biases, and values to the work we do. We hear what our clients say with a particular ear, no more special in its particularity than that of other therapists, but informed by our understanding of women's psychological development as taking a particular form within patriarchal social relations.

From our point of view, one of the corollaries of feminist therapy is that the therapist must believe in a person's open choice of sexual partner. Because of the history and the continuing discrimination against homosexuality in the psychiatric professions it has often been extremely difficult for lesbians to seek psychotherapy. This has been true both for the lesbian in search of individual psychotherapy and for lesbian couples seeking counseling. Feminist therapists need to examine their own deeply held views and possible fears about lesbianism—which may exist even if one is a lesbian and a therapist—in order to work in a clear and unprejudiced way with lesbian clients. Feminist therapists must examine and discuss issues of sexuality within the therapy relationship with both heterosexual and lesbian clients.

Many therapists show their reluctance to do this in fairly obvious ways. Discussing a young adult (an eighteen-year-old) who was attracted to her, Claire, a therapist, herself a lesbian and firmly committed to free sexual expression for lesbians, worried about whether she was influencing her client negatively. As a powerful figure in Melissa's life, encouraging her to share her thoughts and fantasies about loving women, perhaps she was setting her client up for a hard life. Claire considered herself more accepting of lesbianism than "the world out there," and feared that Melissa would get the wrong idea about what she was in for. When Claire looked at her own attitude in supervision she realized that it revealed her own prejudice. To her lesbianism was not simply a choice but a disadvantage. She had come to acknowledge her sexual orientation grudgingly, after hoping for years that she would be happy in a heterosexual relationship. She felt that coming out had its liberating aspects, but it also cut her off from a lot of people. She wasn't sure things had changed so much in the world that being gay was really an accepted alternative. She still felt rage because of discrimination against her and felt the hurt of rejection by her parents. She was afraid Melissa couldn't cope with such upsets. Beyond this, as Claire realized how heterosexuality as an ideal lived inside her, she realized too that she wouldn't have been unduly concerned if a heterosexual therapist had a young adult client who felt a heterosexual attraction for the therapist.

Claire's problem is one of the issues that needs to be thought about and picked up in supervision sessions, so that feminist therapists will not reproduce and pass along sexual prejudices of any sort. Another way such a prejudice can manifest itself is in the kinds of questions a therapist does or does not ask. One client was agonizing about being in a quasihidden lesbian relationship. Part of her felt so distressed about being gay that she would make occasional forays into heterosexuality. She felt somehow that she was deeply inadequate that she wasn't with a man.

THERAPIST: Can you say what is the hardest thing for you to accept—the thing that stands in the way of your embracing your gay identity?

CLIENT: That I have failed ... that I can't seem to get on with men ... Perhaps I don't try properly.

THERAPIST: Has it ever occurred to you that perhaps it is the men who have disappointed you ... that you are not at fault per se?

This intervention opened up a whole new direction for the client. On the surface there was nothing exceptional about the therapist's question. If the client had been talking of a friendship that didn't work out, a therapist might have suggested in a similar way that perhaps the friend was disappointing. But there is often a blind spot around homosexuality, so that typically the therapist will emphasize and pursue a client's inadequacy feelings, thus reinforcing the notion that there is something wrong with homosexuality.

Conscious and unconscious attitudes about class and ethnicity are also felt in the therapy relationship, even when the class and ethnic background of therapist and client are similar. There may be tension on either or both sides about this, and therapists must guard against seeing issues that may well have to do with class and ethnicity only in terms of intrapsychic conflict. (This may derive from the failure by the training instructions to give adequate consideration to class and ethnicity.) Since class and ethnic background are important to who we are and often serve to prohibit certain activities and foster others, unless one is from the appropriate background, a therapist must maintain an awareness of how class and ethnicity affect both her and her view of the client and be ready to explore with the client how and what class and cultural background means in her life at material and psychological levels.

132

Therapists are not always aware that the views they hold are informed by a particular class and ethnic perspective. Because of the power differential in the therapy relationship, the therapist may unwittingly convey such views and thereby influence the therapy in a particular direction. Therapists are constantly evaluating what is happening with their clients in terms of shifts in intrapsychic life and relationships with the world. Awareness of class and ethnic issues is also important if the therapist is to be sensitive, without prejudice, to the life choices that a particular woman makes.

We have found the following points useful in discussing issues of class and ethnicity in postgraduate training workshops at The Women's Therapy Centre:

1. The therapist's treatment goals may be based on her notion of what is appropriate for that class or that ethnic group.
2. The selection of clients is frequently made by criteria that, seemingly value-free, are in fact ideological. Therapists often remark that potential clients are "bright" or "motivated," when what they are responding to is verbal ability and articulateness, which they seem surprised to encounter in working-class women or women from cultures different from their own. Working-class and black people are taken on for therapy more easily if they exhibit middle-class characteristics.
3. Therapists are often blind to the issues of class and race that clients present, perhaps "psychologizing" or interpreting them. Because of this, a therapist may not adequately explore with her clients their ethnic and class backgrounds, thus missing crucial issues for the client.
4. Therapists may be unaware of how their own class and ethnic background contributes to the shape of the therapy and of how it can cause inequalities in the therapy relationship. Therapists may be defensive if they have not explored their own attitudes to class and ethnicity.

133

5. An aspect of psychotherapy training places an emphasis on the difference between "us" (therapists) and "them" (clients). Perhaps therapists utilize class and ethnic differences in this distancing from the client. In addition, in many training programs there is no provision for discussion of issues of class and race, as though they were irrelevant to the personality of the person and unimportant in the therapy. When such issues do come up they are likely to be interpreted exclusively as issues of countertransference and transference, and therefore delegitimated as issues in themselves.

In our workshop we focus on these general themes and then move on to explore our own attitudes. We consider:

1. Our own class and ethnic background and our awareness of it.
2. The background of our own therapist and its role in our own therapy.
3. The background of our supervisor and how it influenced us.
4. The ideas we hold about black, Hispanic, and Asian people, immigrants from Europe, working-class people, Irish people, and therapy.
5. The need to rethink our work with clients in light of the potential tensions that arise around class and ethnicity.

It is vital for the therapist to care for and respect the women she works with. We sense that much training instills a sense of superiority over the client which is revealed in the way cases are discussed in papers and clinical seminars. We feel this often arises because the therapist feels quite genuine concern and sometimes distress at the plight of her client, even when she feels she can be an effective progressive force in her life. Responding to another's painful experiences puts enormous emotional pressure on the therapist, and this is compounded by the therapeutic situation, which does not allow the therapist to share and thus discharge some of her reactions. Instead, she is offered two tools: she can analyze her emotional reactions to her clients within the context of countertransference, and/or fit her clients into a highly evolved diagnostic scheme with a specialist vocabulary.

These two options are valuable and should not necessarily be jettisoned by progressive therapists. What we are concerned with is that these two mechanisms are often the means of changing the therapist's attitude toward the people she sees in therapy from wholesome compassion to faint contempt and alienation. There have been several interesting attempts by feminist therapists to form groups to discuss many of these issues and work against these attitudes. We developed a five-step peer-group supervision model for a conference of psychotherapists held in London in April 1978 (The Feminist Therapist Training Group). In step one, a therapist describes a client she is working with, giving details of her family, her class and ethnic background, her current situation, her sexual orientation, her presenting problems on entering therapy, and the course of the therapy so far. Step two: The therapists share their identification with the client, discussing the areas in the client's life that resemble their own and noting any points in the presentation when the therapists were particularly moved. Step three: We suggest that the therapists ask themselves the following questions: How do they understand the woman's distress? What does this distress have to do with the experience of being a woman? How is her gender central to what she is experiencing? How does the presenting problem or distress relate to her struggle to be an adult woman? Step four: We ask technical questions—How would we work with this particular client? What would the therapy goals be? What is happening in the transference? How would we distinguish between counter-transference, the therapist's transference, and identification? How do we understand the mother-daughter relationship and its developmental implications for girls? We ask for specific suggestions about directions to take the technical innovations. Step five: About a month after the initial discussion the therapist reports to the group on what has happened in the sessions after her first presentation.

In addition to participating in supervisory and consciousness-raising groups, we have found it useful to discuss in study groups, seminars, and informal conversations with each other topics of concern to feminist therapists. For example, a dilemma that confronts us in a particularly stark way is that of how to avoid reproducing the ideological stick of "good mother" in our role as the professional "good mother." Does not the professionalization of women's "giving" skills reach its apex in being a good therapist? Is there not a striking parallel between female socialization and a job in the "helping profession" as a therapist? Both roles require women to help relieve the distress of others, albeit by very different methods.

A way to work on such dilemmas is to discuss them with others who experience them. We have found that clinical seminars devoted to such issues are extremely useful. Such discussions also provide a kind of nurturance that goes against the classic feminine role of giving to the world. For it is essential that as feminist therapists we can find our own sources of support and nurturance.

Notes

1. For the purposes of this book, and in our work supervising the cases of other clinicians, we are using the term countertransference in the following ways: "Countertransference ... as a specific non-neurotic reaction on the part

of the analyst to the transference of the patient. . . . Countertransference is, in fact, the necessary *complement of transference.* Each conditions the other in the sense of a transference–countertransference equation. *They form a functional unity.* . . . The definition offered here thus considers countertransference as a product, as a complement of the transference. It is induced in the analyst by the patient." Michael Lukas Moeller, "Self and Object in Countertransference," *International Journal of Psycho-Analysis* 58 (1977): 365–374.

The classical view of countertransference and a view much in currency today does not distinguish between these aspects of the therapy relationship and the psychotherapists' own transference issues which may be evoked by the client. We find this view too nonspecific to be of technical use, particularly in supervision, and follow Moeller's formulation. As we use countertransference in this sense, it could be argued that the concept of the client's transference needs to be broadened to include the various aspects of self and the experience of the therapist that are evident in the therapy relationship, rather than just the classical narrower formulation of historical transferences. We have not chosen to do this in this book because this idea needs to be more fully worked and elaborated upon.

2. Ibid.

3. Supervision refers to the practice of discussing with a colleague or colleagues one's clinical work in distinct ways: as a monitoring device for technical advice, and as an arena for the exploration of the therapist's countertransference issues.

4. J. Sandler, "Countertransference and Role Responsiveness," *International Journal of Psycho-Analysis* 3 (1976): 43–47.

CHAPTER 7

Women's Psychological Development: Themes and Consequences

HAVING presented our developmental model of women's psychology and having illustrated a feminist approach within the psychotherapeutic setting, we would now like to point to some specific psychological consequences of that development. As we have seen, women's psychology is one of unclear boundaries, of an insecure or illusive sense of self. Women often search for themselves in their relationships with others, seeking definition in contact. The central aspect of women's psychology, the one that embodies most of the major themes, is the lack of psychological separateness, the absence of boundaries within which a secure sense of self is contained.

Girls are taught to be aware of the ways in which their actions affect others, and as a result become cautious about their actions. They almost always bear someone else in mind when they make their decisions about appropriate behavior. When playing in a group of children, we see a little girl go after a favored toy tentatively. As she reaches it she looks around at the reactions of the others to see if she will be stopped. Her assertive behavior is often interrupted by an

138

adult reminding her to be "nice"—that is, to defer to others. Girls rarely experience encouragement and support for gestures of autonomy. More often than not, girls move out into the world accompanied by prohibitions, cautions, restrictions, and fear rather than expectations of success and acceptance. Girls are praised and supported for behavior that expresses concern, thoughtfulness, and care for others. Girls are told they are being selfish when they direct this same energy toward themselves.

Women's second-class position in patriarchal culture is painfully reflected in their psychology. Women do not feel whole; women do not feel confident in themselves; women feel less than equal; women feel like children, not adults; women feel powerless; women feel overdependent; women feel passive; women feel imprisoned by their anger and by the clouds of depression that often surround them. These kinds of feelings are experienced and expressed in many different forms. Feelings of insecurity, unentitlement, abandonment, and anger are distorted and converted into feelings of competition, envy, guilt, and depression, which in turn lead to further self-condemnation. We can remember the feelings of envy which Joyce had when her best friend was accepted to law school. She felt as if Elaine's strengths somehow reflected her own weakness. Feelings of insecurity and unentitlement (not being able to believe that she, too, could be successful in her field) turned to envy and the envy, in turn, led to awful feelings about herself. Joyce was caught in a double bind. On the one hand she had yearnings for achievement and fulfillment, and on the other she was caught by her own internal restraints and prohibitions. Women are caught in an internal world in which their defenses entrap their yearnings for nurturance, acceptance, love, and autonomy.

Using our developmental model we can understand these emotional states by tracing the ways in which they specifically relate to women's experience and to the mother-daughter relationship. Guilt, difficulties with anger, and preponderance of depression in women have their roots in early psychological development and should be viewed from an analysis of women's search for acceptance, for adequate and consistent relating, and for an integrated self.

RoseAnn, a forty-three-year-old woman, described a situation in which she felt her evening was ruined because of the discomfort she felt about her own competitive feelings.

> I hardly knew anyone at the party. A friend from work invited me. I usually feel uncomfortable at parties but I pushed myself to go this time because I know I have to try to meet new people. I was sitting on the couch talking to my friend from work and this other woman she knew, and other people were sitting around in a circle. There was this woman who was talking to two people, a man and a woman, about her work. All I overheard was her saying something about changing departments and finding her work much more interesting and rewarding. I couldn't stop looking over at her. I don't know why, but I kept looking at her, looking at what she was wearing, how she had her hair. I even noticed her nail polish. I started to feel terrible. I felt fat and boring and I could hardly keep up in the conversation I was having. I just wanted to sink into the sofa and hide. I went home early, telling my friend I had to get up very early the next day. When I left I felt really depressed, and I went home and ate.

Why did RoseAnn focus her attention on this other woman? She did not know the woman at all and almost everything she thought about her was fantasy. RoseAnn was anxious about going to the party, wanting to meet new people but frightened at the same time. Focusing on the woman and fantasizing about her was a way for RoseAnn to experience her feelings of insecurity and lack of self-worth. She compared herself to the other woman and found fault with herself every time.

Rather than being able to feel good about herself for her attempt to reach out and meet people, RoseAnn punished herself. She could not accept her fearful feelings—which were absolutely understandable, since she went into a crowd where she knew only one person—and so she condemned herself for not being "perfect" and imagined the other woman to be confident, fearless, beautiful, and content with her life. RoseAnn could not imagine acceptance, although it was what she sought. Unable to feel good about herself, she converted those painful feelings into self-denigrating comparisons and competitiveness in her desire to be as acceptable as she imagined the other woman to be.

One of the important and most obvious ways in which competition between women is expressed is, of course, in the sexual arena. The traditional social requirement that a woman be allied with a man, from whom she will derive her social and personal value (and hence her self-esteem), further requires that she come to see herself as others see her. She extends this critical view of herself to other women both as a comparison and as a threat. When a woman walks into a room full of people she is likely to evaluate the other women automatically and rank herself among them. After the initial physical impression of looks, dress, and probably age, she will take in other attributes of the women she is evaluating—their intellectual activities, their jobs, their sexual arrangements.

This sounds crude and unpleasant, as indeed the experience itself is. Women look at other women who seem "suitably attractive" and imagine that they are comfortable and easy with themselves; each woman wonders how the other has achieved this self-assurance and envies and admires her. Each woman may feel depression or self-hate and hopelessness in relation to the others, while at the same time longing to be in their shoes. Feelings of competition cover the deeper feelings of insecurity. The competitive feelings then produce a new set of feelings of failure, lack of confidence, and inadequacy. Perhaps the most painful aspect of this cycle of insecurity and competition is that women experience these feelings individually and yet they are common to millions of women.

In consciousness-raising groups, women discussed openly for the first time the destructive nature of competition between women and the fact that they are frequently caught in the cycle of competing with each other for men. Women in these groups came to be critical and angry at the society and of course at individual men who promote the competition. Important breakthroughs about the need to support other women reduced feelings of being threatened by each other and thus produced important changes in women's consciousness. Still, competitive feelings were so deep, so dangerous, and now so shameful, that in many groups issues of competition among women remained below the surface.

Failure to deal directly with these uncomfortable feelings often led to the dissolution of women's groups. We have noticed in our clinical work how difficult it is, especially for a self-conscious feminist, to admit that she has competitive feelings toward other women. She will often respond to these feelings with self-punishment and shame because they confirm for her that she is not as strong, self-confident, and independent as she "should" be. There is a new set of rules and "shoulds" that feminists feel they must live by and, although it is now possible for women to struggle to understand and change how they feel and respond, at this point in history it is inevitable that women will feel envious, competitive, and insecure. We cannot ignore our personal histories and the psychologies they have created.

Over the past fifteen years the women's movement has helped women make significant gains in their lives. A woman who chooses to pursue a career is no longer necessarily thought of in male-identified ways, whereas twenty years ago a woman who wanted to advance in her professional work often had to choose between that and a family. Such forced choices are much less frequent today, but along with new freedoms come new pressures. Today women may feel inadequate if their concern is solely in the domestic sphere, raising children and working in the home, because that labor is still much undervalued. Women in greater numbers feel the necessity to pursue a career and then are caught in a dilemma about how to add in having children and a family. These changes have brought feelings of competition to a new level, as women compare themselves to other women and measure their successes both out in the world and in the family. These comparisons reflect women's individual attempts to place themselves, to see where they fit, both in the familiar area and in a world that has not been theirs for long.

Today we not only see competition among women in the pursuit of self-esteem, we also see competitive feelings that arise in a woman who adopts and satisfies ambitions that lie outside those traditionally prescribed for women. A woman who is struggling to fulfill herself by living and working as fully as possible may experience feelings of disloyalty, guilt, and betrayal toward other women. She feels as though she is rejecting an image of femininity deep inside her—divorcing herself from other women.

143

There is a certain safety in the familiarity women feel with their second-class status. It is a connecting link between women. As Simone de Beauvoir puts it in *The Second Sex,* "Women are comrades in captivity for one another, they help one another endure their prison, even help one another prepare for escape."[1] But "escape" from the world of women feels like betrayal.

An example from a six-session workshop on competition illustrates these dynamics. Patty, a songwriter, had just made a tape of a song she had written, and in the first meeting she mentioned her hopes and fears about becoming a professional songwriter. Everybody was very encouraging. Patty came to the second session with news that the song had been sold, but said she felt complicated by it because her roommate, a dancer, was having a difficult time finding any work and envied Patty's good break. Patty did not know how to put together her good feelings about her success and her concern for her friend's situation. In the group we discussed the psychological dilemma that often ensues when one receives something one wants, as shown in Patty's difficulty in feeling her success when it brought her friend's envy. She was trying to push away her own conflicts about digesting her success by focusing on someone else's feeling, when instead she needed to experience her own. Then the two friends could cope together with the differences in their experience without Patty's having to deny or erase her own achievement.

Competitive feelings serve to keep women in their place. Deeply instilled in each woman is an unconscious knowledge of the thresholds that she cannot cross without arousing the anger and envy of other women. In this way women unconsciously collude to keep each other from self-fulfillment. Patriarchy is distilled in each woman's psychology. Competitive and envious feelings prevent her from trying to get what she needs in a society that has a huge stock of prohibitions. Adult women then unknowingly maintain the internal restraints that "protect" them from their wants. A woman's guilt at any wanting keeps her unconsciously connected to the cultural image of femininity. She does not dare break ranks and be separate.

Focusing on the envy of others insured that Patty could not feel wholehearted pleasure in her success. The envy, however, was not merely a figment of Patty's imagination. Her friend did experience feelings of envy. She too was struggling to be recognized and appreciated for her talents, and Patty's acceptance struck a painful chord.

Women do express envy in many situations, and behind the feelings of envy are feelings of longing. A feminist therapist must work with her clients to redirect the energy of their feelings and to look into their feelings of wanting. Behind the envy is a woman's belief that she will never achieve fulfillment, acceptance, or recognition for herself. Envy keeps the focus on other people, on what "they" have rather than what one needs. In our clinical work we often hear therapists talk about envious feelings as an end point: "The client is envious." For us, feelings of envy are a starting point, a conscious feeling that a therapist and client can use as a signpost pointing to a deeper level of meaning. Envy is a common feeling for women because of their knowledge of the impossibility of getting recognition and acceptance for themselves, or of getting approval rather than punishment for self-development.

Feelings of envy and competition are closely linked to feelings of guilt. Women often feel guilty about wanting things for themselves. Guilt has a bad taste and feels disabling, it is a psychological mechanism that appears in the problems of connectedness and separateness.

Let's look at two women's manifestations of guilt, both of them shown in the crucial mother-daughter relationship. One young woman, Jane, does not feel that she has a close relationship with her mother. She finds her mother selfish and unable to give to her daughter in any way. Yet Jane carries feelings of guilt and finds herself telephoning her mother at least once a week. Inevitably she is angry and upset after talking with her mother but this does not stop her from the weekly call. Analyzing Jane's guilt feelings, we learn that Jane feels insecure in the relationship and deeply fears that her mother does not love her. Unconsciously she feels that if she were different, if she had provided her mother with an acceptable daughter to love, then her mother would love her. In her early psychological development, the frustration and rage that Jane experienced in relation to her mother was all mixed up with mother's inadequacy. We can speculate that Jane felt that her bad feelings caused her mother to be the way she was. It becomes Jane's fault that her mother is unloving and Jane feels guilt that her "badness" harmed her mother. Jane's guilt is both about not feeling good enough in herself and about the continuing need for an emotional avenue, a connection, to her mother.

Esther also calls her mother out of guilt, but her guilt is quite different from Jane's. Esther's mother is an immigrant from Eastern Europe who came to the United States in the 1930s and lived in poverty with her husband and two daughters for a number of years. The family came to own a small business and to this day Esther's mother (now in her seventies) still works at the store. Esther is a child psychologist with a Ph.D. She is filled with feelings of guilt about her own life as compared to her mother's. She feels that she should be happy because she has so much in her life, and yet her feelings of guilt prevent her from feeling content. Here again guilt serves the purpose of keeping Esther connected to her mother. For Esther, being psychologically separate would mean being able to feel pain and pride about her mother's life while feeling happy about her own. She would be living in her own shoes and not half her mother's.

Guilt is a chain that binds one person to another out of the impossibility of separateness. For women, asserting their own needs, saying no, makes them feel as though they are pushing another person away. If a woman struggles for her autonomy she may feel as though she is deserting, rejecting, or hurting others; she feels guilty. Because women's boundaries and separateness are unclear, women are particularly susceptible to these feelings of guilt. Guilt therefore, like feelings of competition and envy, blurs a central issue in women's psychology, that of psychological nonseparateness and separateness.

Depression, which often accompanies guilt, is one of the most common psychological distress symptoms. It is frequently treated with psychotropic drugs and mood elevators, but for every woman being treated there is another whose depression goes untreated. The psychiatric profession defines clinical depression in varying ways, and so do people in therapy. The most common description of depression is a feeling of hopelessness; a feeling that one is submerged in gray clouds which one cannot get through, does not have the energy or the desire to even try; one feels lost and cannot imagine ever feeling differently. It is as if one is sunk into a sense of futility where there just isn't much point to anything.

There are two features that emerge from our model of psychological development which, to our minds, shed special light on depression in women. The first is the loss of self[2] that occurs in the early years, when the little-girl inside becomes split off and hidden. The adult woman then carries a sense of hopelessness about ever feeling whole and good within herself, and her depression is a kind of mourning for the lost little-girl. The second feature is a woman's inability to expect a relationship in which she will be seen as herself and accepted and loved. This lack of expectation comes not only from the loss of mother early in the girl's life (as she is trained to become like her mother, the caregiver, and pushed toward heterosexuality, to turn from her mother to a man) but from the loss of any *expectation* for continued maternal nurturance from any motherlike person who might provide emotional support and understanding. The depressed woman feels that she is surviving within a gloomy, one-dimensional existence, that she has lost the part of herself which had a spark, a need, a desire for contact and activity. People seem even farther away than they were before and she feels paralyzed, unable to decrease the distance.

Annette is forty-six, has been married to John for twenty-two years, and has three children. She has had periods of depression since she was a teenager. Her family refers to such a period as "one of those moods" and treats her gingerly at those times. John doesn't know what he can do to help and finds himself getting angry with her when she's depressed. When he asks her if there's anything bothering her, she just shrugs and sighs, and so he leaves her alone. Annette was the elder of two children, two years older than Anthony. Annette's memories of her childhood are mostly of spending her days with her mother at home and trying to amuse herself by escaping into a world of fantasy games. She remembers feeling very angry with Anthony and being scolded by her mother for her anger. She was often told to leave Anthony alone, not to bother him, to go play in her own room. Anthony was the special child. The family was proud of having a boy and he was treated with great care and concern. Annette grew up feeling a tremendous amount of rage toward both Anthony and her mother. She felt that her mother had abandoned her when Anthony was born. Because of her own feelings about herself and because of her identification with her daughter, Annette's mother was never able to be a "good enough"[3] mother to Annette. Even before Anthony was born, she was a somewhat frightened and insecure little girl, tentative in her demands for fear of her mother's anger. The insecurity she felt about herself and her relationship to her mother was only compounded by her brother's birth. In her fantasy games her rich internal world excelled. Here she felt a sense of control: she could make things happen as she wanted them to.

Annette's depression was a result of turning her anger against herself—she was remarkably skilled at doing so—and of mourning for the little-girl part of herself that had been shut away for as long as she could remember. As an adult Annette could not express her anger to others because it felt too explosive. She felt that her anger was such that if she let it out she would obliterate the other person. Her need for contact and relationships would not let her risk losing a relationship by expressing her anger. When she suffered disappointments in relationships these incidents resounded for her internally, bringing to the forefront the loss of her little-girl self, her suffocation by her own anger, and her sense of hopelessness and futility about her situation. These feelings changed in the course of her therapy. There were two central components of the therapy which alleviated Annette's feelings of depression. First, Annette's anger was expressed in the therapy and was accepted and validated. The anger she felt, at times, toward her therapist did not harm the therapist or destroy the therapy relationship. Second, Annette felt for the first time that she was seen in her entirety and still cared for by her therapist. It took a very long time for her to trust that her therapist's care and concern was genuine, but she did come to feel that she was capable of being loved for herself.

Because of the internal psychological split between the little-girl inside and the adult woman facing the world, many women suffer depression from a sense that no one will ever really see them whole. The discrepancy between the way others see them and the way they see themselves brings a sense of futility and hopelessness. Not all difficulties with anger result in depression, but women's difficulty with anger is often a thread in their depression.

Both girls and boys have to deal with psychological restrictions and fears about anger hurting or destroying their needed and loved caregivers, as we saw in chapter 2. Girls, however, also learn that anger is not an acceptable feminine characteristic, and this is why women have so much difficulty with this emotion. They find their own anger ugly. They are ashamed of it, find it hard to express, and fear it will hurt others. They are also afraid of other people's anger. Thus women often swallow their anger and either turn it back on themselves in one way or another or express it indirectly. For many women feelings of anger are so taboo, so frightening, that they themselves are unaware that they are feeling or expressing it.

Anger can be a straightforward and direct emotional communication between people. But like envy, guilt, and competitiveness, anger can be understood in a more complex way as a defense. In psychotherapy we frequently see how both denial of anger and persistent holding on to angry feelings toward another person are connected to the themes of deprivation and lack of separateness. Behind feelings of anger lie even more painful feelings of disappointment and despair. Not exposing the anger and disappointment stokes the fantasy of the other person being able to make everything better. The anger keeps the connection. It fuels the hope that the person one is angry with will actually come through.

Lisa is married to James. She often feels angry with him and yet she has only expressed her anger two or three times in their six years of marriage. She says she is afraid of his response. He might be angry with her for being angry, or make her feel wrong or "crazy" for being angry in the first place, or turn his back on her and cut her off emotionally. She feels that she'd rather swallow her angry feelings than go through the pain of the scenario she imagines. Instead, Lisa expresses her anger indirectly by turning off sexually. She feels tired, uninterested, closed off.

By holding onto her anger and keeping it inside, Lisa is unconsciously protecting herself from other, more painful feelings. In tracing the times that Lisa felt the most anger toward James, we saw that they were times when he disappointed her. For example, when Lisa had her first appointment with an obstetrician she mentioned to James that she would like him to come along and he said he would. On the day of the appointment he phoned to say that something had gone wrong at his office and he had to stay and straighten things out. He told her he was sorry and would see her later at home. As he talked Lisa felt as if she were crumbling inside. She wanted to cry, but she merely dropped her voice almost to a whisper and said that it was all right and she'd see him later. After the moment of feeling enormously upset, Lisa became angry, and her anger grew throughout the afternoon until she dreaded seeing James that evening. When he got home and asked what had happened at the doctor's, Lisa merely mumbled that everything was fine and

151

talked as little as possible for the rest of the evening. Later that night, in bed, she continued the cold shoulder literally, curling up in a ball on her side of the bed and turning off the light.

If we go back to the time of the phone call, we can see that there were about thirty seconds during which Lisa was able to experience her real feelings of disappointment. She wanted James to be with her both physically and emotionally and she felt abandoned by him on both levels. (That evening she would abandon him in the same way, thus unconsciously trying to communicate to him what she felt by making him feel it.) Remaining in touch with those feelings was too painful and also left her emotionally open to James. She could not allow herself to be in the very vulnerable position of still needing James when he would not be there. Anger came in as a protective defense against the feelings of disappointment and abandonment and the even worse feeling that James was not with her emotionally. The anger, therefore, helped to maintain her connection to him.

In therapy Lisa also revealed that deep down she hadn't felt entitled to ask James to go with her to the obstetrician. Asking for that support was asking for too much. This is a common feeling for many women and brings us to another consequence of women's psychological development—their difficulties with receiving.

All women know that in order to receive they must give. Giving is something a woman learns early. It is a survival tool, a deeply rooted part of her psychic structure and experience of self, and the price she pays for economic security. But a woman who has suppressed much of her need to receive unconsciously feels that deep inside she has only a hungry part of herself that wants to take; she feels that she has nothing to give. One of the ways this wanting plays out is through the woman's feeling that she is unjustified in receiving attention. Only after a woman has given something to the other person does she feel justified in taking. If someone is kind, concerned, and receptive, the woman feels the urge to repay a hundredfold. Being given to purely because she is deserving is often confusing and moving for a woman because she does not conceive of herself in this way. She so anticipates annoyance and rejection if she displays her needs that being given attention takes her by surprise.

A woman who experiences being given to when she feels she has not given first, or will not have the opportunity to return the giving, may react with distrust. Why is someone giving to her unless something is wanted in return? One client, Jackie, met a woman she liked in one of her classes. They had coffee together and exchanged phone numbers. The following week the woman called Jackie just for a long telephone chat, and after they hung up Jackie spent a good deal of time wondering why the woman really called, and what she had really wanted. Jackie could not believe her acquaintance genuinely liked her and was interested in her for the person she was.

One of the consequences of this painful and complicated dynamic of giving and receiving can be seen in women's experience of sex. Paradoxically, many women report a fear of being satisfied and given to. When there is a chance for their own needs to be met, the experience is so unfamiliar that it may produce conflict with the ingrained notion that women must defer to others' needs. Even when the opportunity presents itself with a willing and giving lover, it may be terribly difficult for a woman to ask for or take sexual pleasure. Many women find it easier to give sexual pleasure to a partner. Receiving feels like too much is being given. A woman is often caught in a double bind; on the one hand she finds it difficult to assert her needs, and yet deep down she may feel resentful that she is not being given to. She may feel anger at both herself and her lover for the situation in which she is preoccupied with satisfying his or her needs and not her own.

Another difficulty that women have in the sexual situation is actually being in the experience rather than being spectators of their own experience. A woman may feel that she is there *for* her lover and see herself through her lover's eyes. Once again we see a woman not being in her own skin, involved with her own needs and pleasure, but rather involved in the needs and pleasure of another, with her own unmet needs providing the basis from which she gives. Her shaky boundaries and her yearnings for maternal nurturance mean that she is always striving to be close to others in the hope of feeling whole. Her sense of safety within herself is ambiguous.

In her sexual relationship a woman may look to a lover to give her a sense of completeness. She yearns to connect with another person, to be loved and held. And once again she is faced with a dilemma because of her feelings of fear and shame about her sexuality.

Woman everywhere is viewed in her relationship to her sexuality. Feminist commentators have drawn attention to the dichotomous ways in which women are seen and experience themselves and their sexuality. One side of the dichotomy is the image of the virgin princess, father's untouched daughter and possession. The woman is pure, naïve, expectant, and adoring; she will give herself to the right man, but her body is more spiritual than carnal. On the other side of the dichotomy is the image of the woman who is actively sexual, perhaps bewitching, Mata Hari or the whore, ravenous and rapacious and very exciting. The woman who stands outside the family, the single woman, the woman who is not attached within a sexual relationship, represents women's unharnessed sexuality. She carries an aura that both men and women respond to with awe and fear; she represents a threat to the given order.

But whichever side of the dichotomy the woman pursues in an expression of her womanhood, or if she attempts to straddle both images, her sexuality is always formed with an idea of the image she can create. For female sexuality is not simply experienced by the woman as an aspect of herself that she can enjoy and communicate; it is, because of her social position, both a product for herself and her product in the world. Women's sexuality has been a means by which women have found their place, whatever their social class or ethnic background. The paradox of female sexuality being the vehicle for a woman to find a home, so to speak, and yet once she has found that home needing to hide her sexuality or channel it into producing babies, means that all women live with the split of simultaneously having to be sexual and yet having to curb their sexuality.

Because of the psychic nonseparation from mother and mother's injunctions about female sexuality a woman may find that her attachment to mother is expressed in unwittingly "taking her into the bedroom." The daughter feels guilt in her attempts to connect with another and unconsciously feels she has abandoned mother.

At a psychic structural level the nonseparated nature of women's ego may mean that sexual connection with a partner brings with it a fear of loss of self. During sexual activity a woman is experiencing the prominence of the sensual and erotic thread in human connection. Her sexuality flows through her body and connects with another's. Other forms of communication, such as language, conscious thinking processes, and discourse, move into the background. This deeply gratifying sensual communication is an adult ideal. But women's false boundaries—as well as those of men, which arise from their defensive separation from mother at separation-individuation—make this form of communication problematic.

The woman, unsure of her boundaries, may feel unable to get out of her head and into her body; or she may feel taken over in the sexual merger. To have a pleasurable and satisfying sexual experience one must be able to let go, and to merge with another one must have a defined sense of self to return to. Because adult sexuality echoes aspects of mother-infant preverbal sensuality in its very unique communication, sexuality and merger may stir up deeply resonant early physical experience before there was a definite sense of self and before language. For many women the melting of physical boundaries is a terrifying prospect. They feel they will be engulfed by a lover and will lose themselves.

Notes

1. Simone de Beauvoir, *The Second Sex,* New York, 1952, p. 575.
2. Our own account crosses interestingly with Alice Miller's theoretical approach to depression as relating to loss of self. See *Prisoners of Childhood,* New York, 1981.
3. D. W. Winnicott developed the concept "good enough mothering" to describe a mother's ability to satisfactorily provide a loving and holding environment for her infant.

CHAPTER 8

Phobias and
Somatic Symptoms

These are women who came from an atmosphere where they had to grow up in a hurry. They had little opportunity for genuine self-expression, especially of warmer feelings. They may have had great compassion for the suffering of others, but very little sympathy for their own. As girls they were capable and self-reliant, but were not really whole.

ALEXANDRA SYMONDS
"Phobias After Marriage: Women's
Declaration of Dependence"

SOME psychological symptoms affect only women and some affect both women and men, although almost always in disproportionate numbers. Vast numbers of women suffer with both somatic and phobic symptoms.[1] In a curious way, many of these have been accepted as almost legitimate forms of letting the world know that all is not right. At the same time such symptoms are often hidden. Certain debilities, those that are not seen as reducing women's ability to function in the role society has assigned, may even be encouraged in indirect ways; they keep women in their place.

The constraints that surround a woman's life may cloud

157

the fact that she, for example, cannot travel or is non-orgasmic. A woman's symptoms, like so much of her inner experience of self, are frequently out of view. As we describe various symptoms—phobias, obsessions, anorexia, and compulsive eating—we will refer to our general model of women's psychological development and discuss the symptoms as expressions of internal struggles related to a woman's little-girl self and the structure of her psyche. First, however, we may remind ourselves that women's social position has meant that a woman's major sphere of influence and areas for self-expression are confined to the home. Her home has to a large extent been synonymous with her notion of her valid world. As we have seen, women's psychological development dovetails with the requirements of their social role. They are brought up to be connected to others and then to attend to and defer to their needs. But the psychic preparation for this social role leaves a woman with a legacy of unmet needs, frustrated desires, deep feelings of unentitlement, and a fragmented, malleable, or incomplete sense of self. These experiences in turn generate feelings of anger, despair, and hopelessness. Women unable to reconcile themselves with their confinement attempt to break out. Such attempts may be conscious and purposeful, or unconscious, or both. An unconscious expression of such protest, rage, or desperation often manifests itself in a somatic or phobic symptom.

Phobias

A phobic reaction to a particular object or event is a terrorizing and fearful experience in which the person feels utterly helpless. Known ways of being seem elusive and one is overwhelmed by unfamiliar sensations, "unreality feelings," and visual distortions. These experiences are so draining and unpleasant that once outside of them the person thinking about them is often unable to imagine that she will survive a repetition of the experience. A woman who has a phobic reaction to riding in an elevator, for example, is terrified at the idea of having to enter one and be in one. The idea of having to go through with it paralyzes her and feels absolutely impossible. She cannot conceive of being able to live past the experience.

The onset of a phobia is usually unexpected. The individual so affected often has had no previous experience of being in psychological distress. We see many women in therapy who have become phobic or in other ways symptomatic only in adult life. In fact, the phobia is often the reason they begin therapy. They may start out having an anxiety attack in an elevator or subway or while they are driving. They then become fearful of such a panic overtaking them again and try to avoid elevators, subways, or cars. There are women with multiple phobias, women with just one type of phobia, and women who have shifting phobias or phobias that come out only under acute circumstances. Some phobias are only infrequently or momentarily disabling. For example, a woman who does not like birds can avoid them—by staying away from parks—in a fairly straightforward way. In our practice, however, we have worked with many women whose fear is with them on a fairly continual basis—women who feel incapacitated by a phobia.

Phobias can be understood as defense structures within the psyche. Negative experiences such as the rejection in the push-pull dynamic are extremely painful. For instance, they create in the little-girl—later the woman—the feeling that she herself is bad. This feeling is so intolerable that the person can hardly cope with it. Such powerful and uncontainable feelings are pushed out of consciousness and gravitate toward the unconscious, where they become inaccessible and repressed.

This phenomenon of splitting and repressing bad feelings combines with projection, another mechanism of the psyche. Projection is the process of unconsciously placing a part of oneself or feelings one has outside oneself, onto another person or object. Phobias can be understood by grasping the two concepts of splitting and projection. For example, Alison is angry but is fearful of her anger. Without realizing it she projects this anger onto John and thinks and experiences John as angry. In other words she sees her own angry feelings in him. Her feelings have become detached from her own experience and reattached elsewhere. Alison then has a reaction to John's "angry" feelings. She may be afraid of them; she may admire his capacity to feel all right about being angry; she may goad him to express them. Her feelings are searching for expression now in a new and unpredictable area. If John is coincidentally angry, Alison may get some relief by his being able to recognize and express his anger. Seeing herself in his shoes gives her some measure of satisfaction. However, if John is not angry, she will feel frustrated and confused and distant from her own feelings.

What happens in a phobia is that a woman is trying to separate unacceptable internal feelings from herself and dispose of them onto something outside herself. Unaware that these feelings live inside her, she experiences the "something else" as the source of upset. The train, the plane, the spider embodies the bad feelings she has thrown onto it and the danger now exists in the world in a particular form rather than within her. The bad feelings have been discharged and placed outside of the person rather than simply repressed. With the badness now firmly contained in an outside object, the woman gathers a fleeting security and a temporary distance from distress. If we remember Ruth from chapter 1 (page 19) we will recall that, although she was persistently disappointed in her contact with her mother, she continued to need her and want her. She found it hard to keep in her consciousness the complex of feelings this stirred up in her in relation to her unmet needs. When she was twenty-four, Ruth moved away from the city her mother lived in. She looked forward to their visits and she approached her mother optimistically. She was always "shocked" when she was let down and disappointed by her. A couple of years later, Ruth became phobic and found herself unable to travel, even to her mother's, without a companion. In effect, Ruth erected a psychic wall to keep out her negative feelings about herself, which arise from her coping with her feelings of being unlovable. For the phobic woman, the bad feelings she has about herself are so overwhelming that she cannot come near them. They represent such self-hate and conviction of unworthiness that they are hard to approach and dissect. In a therapeutic relationship the bad object relations they express can be explored because that relationship creates the conditions in which the split-off experiences can be slowly and safely integrated.

Generally, the onset of a phobia is triggered by one or a series of bad situations in the external world, such as the loss of a loved one or the loss of critical elements in one's emotional security. Such a loss then creates a situation of internal collapse. If a woman's relationships have been providing her sense of security, a significant loss destroys her illusory sense of well-being and throws her into a state of being with herself and her "bad" internal relations.

Let us look at the psychological structure of such a woman to see why she comes to be susceptible to her phobias. In

her early development the woman has not experienced sufficient and consistent nurturing and so she has not embodied
a solid sense of self. She has not *felt* the empathetic containment that allows one to know that upsetting feelings and
experiences can be gone through and tolerated. The phobic
woman has experienced extreme inconsistency in early relating and she has not embodied enough security and love. Her
psychic structure is fragile. Because she has not developed a
confidence or sense of sureness about her existence, it feels
precarious. She does not have the capacity to reassure herself
or soothe herself. When she is flooded by bad feelings, her
already fragile self almost seems to dissolve psychically; her
capacity to mediate painful feelings disappears and she
would collapse psychically if she did not project these feelings out from herself. Initially, then, the phobia acts in a
protective sense, keeping the feelings of badness at some distance. However, as the symptom persists the woman may
come to feel ashamed and upset about this disability and
then the bad feelings and upset catch up with her. The phobia surrounds her and she cannot escape.

There are several points about phobias that are essential
for the therapist to understand. All phobic people have this
in common: they are terribly frightened by their feelings and
they communicate this fear powerfully in the therapy. It is
most important that the therapist not be put off or alarmed
by the fear and anxiety the client transmits, but instead convey a confidence that slowly and gradually she can help the
client explore the meaning of the phobic response and deal
with the feelings—the deeper, central fears—that have
evoked it. The woman feels out of control of the terrifying
feelings; at any moment they could completely overwhelm
her and reduce her to a state of panic. Indeed, many women
describe phobias as "panic attacks." Some women compart-

mentalize the phobias in such a way that only certain situations bring on the panic, such as traveling by subway or crossing bridges. These women may have no real experience of themselves as being in psychological distress but merely feel they have a peculiar reaction to the specific activity. For other women the experience of distress may be more acute. They may continuously experience terror of being taken over by the badness and disintegrated feelings. This is often the fear behind the phobia. The woman fears that, stranded in terror, she will actually fall apart.

When we look for the actual meaning of specific phobias it is important to explore the range of meanings for the woman concerned. For example, when a woman has a transportation phobia—and these phobias are very common among women—what is it that she is terrified of? Is it moving from one place to another? Is it being in transit? Is it being trapped? Is it being suspended on a bridge with no platform? If a woman cannot go from point A to point B, it may be that she cannot leave point A; that she cannot leave the security, however unsatisfactory, that she has found there. Or it may be that she cannot cope with a new situation; she does not expect a new situation to have anything good to offer because her previous experiences have been so unsatisfactory.

Many phobic women, however, lack internal continuity and feel that to move from point A to point B is to risk losing themselves. One fear we have heard expressed many times is that it is not reaching point B or leaving point A that is the difficulty, it is being trapped in a situation (such as the train or a plane) that makes the woman feel that she has no self, that she will go "mad." Symbolically being in the plane represents her lack of control over her emotions and her vulnerability; she is in one sense alone and trapped with her depleted self. She cannot escape and at the same time she must entrust herself to others. She is caught in the plane with all the bad feelings threatening to suffocate her. In this kind of phobic reaction the psychic concentration is on protecting a fragile inner self that feels discontinuous.

This is different in kind from another fairly common airplane phobia that centers not on being trapped but on crashing. In such a phobia the woman fears that she has given up her power to make things safe. She has handed herself over to a perhaps unreliable pilot/caregiver whom she must trust. Her fate is in his or her (usually his) hands. She does not have the power to affect the outcome. Whatever she does it is up to him. This situation makes her extremely anxious and she may engage in all sorts of peripheral activities hoping they will make the situation safe. For example, she may fly only on certain kinds of planes or at particular hours. By making such choices she feels less passive and out of control. She feels her activities, her decisions, are affecting the outcome of the flight. Psychically she refuses to yield power entirely to another because that experience feels too dangerous.

The existence of false boundaries in the psychology of women can be most dramatically seen in the symptom of agoraphobia. Ninety-five percent of agoraphobics are women. What we have to understand is why a particular woman is frightened to leave her home. What does she fear? Is it leaving home base? Is the home the only safe place for her? Is it arriving somewhere else? Is it being with other people? Is it being alone in the world? There is a different meaning for each of these possibilities, and the meaning is related to the particular woman's psychic development and her defense structure. For agoraphobic women the boundaries of home are substitutes for psychological boundaries. She has had to create false boundaries because the possibility of genuine separateness was not available to her in her development. A woman may fear that if she steps outside the house she will lose the physical boundaries she has come to rely on and hence she will lose herself. Many women who are agoraphobic also have allied feelings of claustrophobia. The false external boundaries not only serve to contain and "protect" the woman; at the same time they also trap her. Once again the woman suffers by being surrounded by and unable to get away from her distress. Agoraphobia and claustrophobia are representations of the psychic prison the woman is in.

Some women become phobic after marriage, when they have left their parents' home and are making a life with a partner of their choice. On the face of it marriage provides a woman with the possibility of a consistent loving partner. Myths about romantic love hold out the possibility that in marriage one will at last be understood, met, and cherished. Of course many women and men find their marriages fulfilling, but for a woman whose psychic structure is unintegrated, marriage may jar psychically because it dispels, at an unconscious level, the fantasy that she can find the acceptance in her partner that she has searched for from her mother (see chapter 9). This may be so devastating that it is in itself a sort of loss. The destruction of the fantasy that finally she will be met creates an internal collapse. She becomes phobic as a defense against the despair and depression that ensue. Symbolically her phobia reveals her dependency needs and her wish for connectedness. It proclaims her inability to carry on in the old ways. It is a cry for help. But she may be so ashamed of the phobia, and so self-contemptuous if it persists, that neither she nor her partner will hear the kernel of its message—that she has not been allowed to be dependent.

Phobias after marriage may also be triggered by loving

relationships. Such a relationship may be psychically disconcerting if it is in strong contrast with what a woman has become habituated to. She may have longed for a close relationship but be overwhelmed by its actuality because it brings up all the hidden feelings of rage, loss, and hurt caused by disappointment with her original love object, and it exposes the hidden little-girl. If the woman cannot contain these feelings they become somaticized. The new intimacy may also release the unconscious desire for merger and dissolve a woman's false boundaries so that she "merges" with her partner. She takes his boundaries for her own and wants to be with him all the time. A phobia may then represent her need to be cared for—she cannot travel, or she must stay at home—and at the same time keep her in psychological isolation. Her attachment may highlight her need for the other person, so that actual, external separation becomes impossible. The phobia is a symptom of her difficulty with being separate because she was not allowed to be sufficiently dependent in early life.

A symptom that illustrates the somaticization of boundary problems very directly is vaginismus, the involuntary tightening of vaginal muscles that prevents penetration. One way to understand vaginismus is to see it as expressing a woman's fear of being taken over, of being invaded and losing herself. Having a shaky sense of her psychological boundaries, she must protect the only boundary she knows, her physical body. Unconsciously she perceives sexual intercourse as the penetration of her boundaries, an invasion of herself. Vaginismus is a physical expression of the creation of false boundaries in an attempt to maintain or build a sense of self. The rigid boundaries expressed through the closing of the vagina prevent merger because merger means disintegration and loss of self in the other.

166

Obsessional Anxieties

In our clinical practice we often encounter the symptom of obsessional anxieties. For example, a woman leaving her house may have to return to check that she has turned off the gas or locked the door ten times before she feels safe in her departure. Another may need to scrub her pots and pans an increasing number of times to feel satisfied that they bear no traces of dirt. For some women it is not an actual activity that needs to be constantly redone but rather that they are in the grip of a mental set piece, or a series of mental rituals that once started up have to be finished before they can go on to the next thing. These rituals vary from person to person. One woman may need to review in detail the last conversation she had with the person she is about to see. She works it over and over in her mind, making sure that she wasn't pushy, rude, or unkind. She is guilty all the time about her negative feelings and she soothes herself with the knowledge that she has not exposed any negative thoughts. Another woman may find herself involved in a counting ritual. She counts each step she takes in a series of threes and then the threes into a further series. Before she arrives at her destination she has to have arithmetically solved the threes in a predecided scheme or else she cannot proceed.

These symptoms are no more under voluntary control than phobias. However much effort a woman makes to intercede she cannot cut into the obsession. It invades her and she is drawn to carry out the thoughts or activities it signals. When she is not directly obsessing she may feel tremendously encumbered or humiliated by the obsession. As a result she may be loath to talk about it in general or even in therapy.

When a woman is constantly drawn to repetitive thoughts

or internal dialogues, the obsession expresses her difficulties with relating and trusting in relationships that are truly interactive. Her inner thoughts are compelling, absorbing, and relatively reassuring because they follow certain patterns and cover a psychological terrain that is knowable and controllable. They can be relied on in a way that relationships in which one is vulnerable cannot. Because the fears and difficulties contained within the actual obsession are successfully confronted, they provide a haven from disappointing relationships. The end of an obsessive episode provides a certain reassurance and calmness.

A psychological developmental explanation for these obsessions can be found if we remind ourselves of how in early development the infant takes difficult experiences into herself and tries to change them round by having a different relationship to her internal objects. This same psychic phenomenon occurs in obsessions. For example, a woman feels upset about a particular situation. Consciously or unconsciously she feels out of control. She gets obsessed with thinking about the situation or another one it reminds her of. She mulls it over in her mind and tries to make it work out in a different way. She works it over and over, listing it, thinking about it, trying to change it, getting caught up in trying to transform what she has experienced or expects to experience. Because she does not feel that she has any control over changing it in reality, she attempts to do all the changing inside her head. As the woman becomes increasingly caught up with trying to manipulate the situation internally, she avoids the painful feelings that arose from the initial reality of the difficult situation.

A woman who has to keep checking that she has locked her front door or turned off the gas, for instance, is constantly confronting the question of whether she is safe and whether she can look after herself. Her obsessive activity symbolizes her dilemma. She must take care of herself for there is no one else, and yet she fears she isn't able to do so straightforwardly. In therapy we try to address this dilemma. We want to help the woman explore the painful experience that she is trying to transform internally and get away from. We look at the way in which her dependency desires were thwarted and try to meet her current needs within the therapy relationship.

Eating Problems: Compulsive Eating, Bulimia, and Anorexia

Compulsive eating, bulimia, and anorexia are related to each other and share certain specific manifestations. They affect a great number of women and are on the increase. Compulsive eating has been estimated to affect 60 percent of the female population between the ages of fifteen and forty-five. Two in a hundred school girls in the U.S.A. exhibit anorectic tendencies and 50 percent of female college students are estimated to have bulimic episodes. The statistics can only be approximate for two reasons. First, all these eating problems have a hidden aspect to them, as compared to obesity, which can be fairly well documented; and second, it is only recently that their increase in the population has brought them into view as serious psychological problems.

Women's traditional social position means that a woman's body is one of her primary assets in the world, for with it she attracts a man who then provides her with a home and a family and social legitimation.[2] A woman's body is integral to her attaining the position of wife and mother. At the same time, as we know, certain aspects of a woman's life inevitably cause conflict which it may be impossible to express. The distress a woman feels, the conflicts she experiences, the taboos against her longings often show themselves, not surprisingly, in her body. A woman may unconsciously express her distress through the way she relates to food. Women who are affected by compulsive eating problems eat in such a way that they are out of touch with the physiological cues that signal hunger and satisfaction. As these mechanisms are repressed, eating and food take on a whole complex of psychological meanings.

A compulsive eater may alternate between eating in a fairly rigid fashion that denies or limits the kind or amount of food she has, and binge eating in which she ingests large quantities of foods that she does not allow herself during her more restricted periods. This way of relating to food leads to self-disgust and recrimination, which in turn propels the woman into further episodes of bingeing or renewed efforts at deprivation. Simultaneously the compulsive eating expresses an obsessive attempt to change one's body size. The woman imagines that if her body size were different her problems would disappear. Just as in any obsession she may think her body size—the object of her obsession—to be the problem. In reality it is not, of course, but is a screen for other troubling issues. The social background of compulsive eating problems and the desire to change one's body size has been discussed elsewhere;[3] here we will concentrate on how these pressures are expressed in developmental psychological terms. In compulsive eating a woman is expressing both a fundamental need for soothing and a sense that at a very basic level she is not able to be appropriately responsive to her own needs. The woman is distanced from her own body in the same way that she is in disjuncture with her emotional needs. Her attempts to go toward food express her neediness, her desire to get. Her moves toward food are always a positive attempt to affirm a need, but the historical conditions under which her needs have not been met mean that at the same moment she reaches toward the nurturance—the food—she is not able to believe that it is all right for her either to want or to get. The food symbolizes comfort and holding, but it is a somewhat treacherous comforter because it does not provide the kind of satisfaction she craves. Every week or so for some women, daily for others, this ritual of going for soothing and being disappointed is played out, leaving the woman with feelings that confirm her sense of unentitlement and deprivation.

Just as other defenses are used to cover the needy little-girl inside, compulsive eating too is a protective mechanism. Compulsive eating behavior expresses a woman's fear that nobody will give to her; that she cannot get what she wants; that she has not had enough; that she will be insatiable. The compulsive eater is attempting to nurture herself, however painfully she goes about it. There is at some unconscious level an acknowledgment of need, yet when a woman is eating compulsively she is pushing down that need at an emotional level. Women who have compulsive eating problems attach tremendous significance to different body states. For many of them being thin is a consciously desired goal. Thinness represents all that is good, healthy, and sexual, while fatness symbolizes sadness, isolation, and self-hate. Unconsciously, however, these body states often express quite different meanings, which begins to explain a compulsive eater's difficulty in reaching or remaining at her "ideal" size. For example, thinness can mean vulnerability or perfection, fatness is a shield and a protection. For a compulsive eater, being thin and giving up the fat represents starving—starving emotionally, having needs exposed and unmet. Her needs will be visible, her deprivation will be uncovered. It is as if, without the protective cover of her fat, her neediness will scream out. In developmental terms, then, the fat hides her little-girl. It creates an outside physical boundary that covers the little-girl and separates that part of her from the world.

Bulimic women have similar kinds of ideas attached to body states. The main characteristic of bulimia is the intense cycle of bingeing and purging great quantities of food that occurs daily, or in many instances several times daily. The woman is drawn to eat but is unable to keep inside of her the food and nourishment she so badly wants. She takes the food in furtively and hurriedly, knowing as she eats it that she will bring it up and feel a kind of release. She is caught in a terrible tension of wanting and not being allowed to have.

The anorectic woman eats compulsively in a binge from time to time and sometimes brings her food up. However, her relationship to food is characterized by an obsessive interest and a steadfast avoidance of taking in any more than very tiny amounts. In anorexia a woman is attempting to split off the painful experiences she has had and is currently having. She cannot tolerate her feelings. She experiences her emotional life as an attack on herself, and she attempts to control it so that she will not be devoured by her emotions. She tries to gain control over her body and mind by creating an altogether new person inside herself. As she rejects her needy, hungry, yearning self and tries to subject it to extreme rules and regulations, she is trying to create a persona for herself that she finds acceptable. She may adopt an extreme regime of diet and exercise in which, for example, she has to run several miles each day, or perhaps engage in strenuous exercise in order to sit down for half an hour. In turn, submission to the exercises creates a boundary between the woman and her needs, so that she feels a sense of strength, but it is a false strength because it is dependent on her vigilance and is in danger of collapse at any time. To maintain this strength she must deny herself, and in the denying create a person she can admire: *a person who appears to have no needs and no appetites.*

The anorectic woman relates to her body as she relates to her emotional life. At certain points in her life her body has shown itself to be outside her control by producing menstrual periods, breasts, hips. Her body insists, "Here I am. I'm changing. You can't control me," and she feels, "Yes, I can control you, I will transform you. I will not have breasts, I will not have hips, and I will not have periods. I will not be a woman. I will not be like you, mother. I will not reproduce your life and I will not take in your food. I will not take you inside of me, I will make myself into something else, something other than you." In trying to gain control over her body and emotions and gain a sense of self-worth, she institutes rules that she then holds onto and keeps to religiously, but at the same time she is depriving herself of food and thereby causing herself harm. She tries to split off the "bad" part of herself and give herself something good—the rules and regulations and an unneedy self-image—to hold on to. But as she tries to control the feeling part of her, she is destroying her body. Tragically and paradoxically, in her struggles for control over herself she may actually lose herself.

Anorectics do intermittently rebel against their self-imposed strictures, and this is often expressed in bingeing.[4] Unfortunately, they cannot keep the food they allow themselves; they have to purge themselves of it, by laxatives or by vomiting. Yet the part of the anorectic woman that initiated the binge was attempting to get nurturance, food, love, and life. It is this part, which is struggling toward life, that the therapist can catch hold of and work with.

When working clinically it is most important to understand the symbolic meanings of body states for compulsive eaters, bulimics, and anorectics. It is also important to realize that these expressions of eating disorders can be full-time obsessions, and we remember that obsessions are distractions from the real underlying feelings of distress. They are attempts at solutions to painful problems. In anorexia, bulimia, and compulsive eating, what we see are women trying to change the shapes of their lives by trying to change the shapes of their bodies.

Notes

1. Joy Melville quotes studies which show that 95 percent of agoraphobics are women. See *Phobias and Obsessions,* London, 1977. Men's symptoms are likely to appear in distinctly different, more directly somatic patterns, such as ulcers and heart attacks. By contrast, in our clinical experience and informal observations obsessional anxieties seem to be evenly divided between the sexes.

2. See Susie Orbach, *Fat Is a Feminist Issue* and *Fat Is a Feminist Issue II,* New York, 1978, 1982.

3. Ibid. This is still deeply felt by many, many women in spite of today's expanding options. Preoccupation with body image and dissatisfaction with one's own body are so common that they seem taken for granted as aspects of being a woman.

4. There is a great range of anorectic behavior. See John Sours, M.D., *Starving to Death in a Sea of Objects,* Jason Aronson, New York, 1980. Some anorectics regularly binge and purge while others do not have these cycles at all. For a discussion of anorexia from a feminist perspective, see Susie Orbach, "The Psychotherapist and Anorexia," *British Journal of Medicine,* July 1981.

CHAPTER 9

Dynamics Between Couples and Implications for Couple Counseling

INCREASING knowledge of women's psychology has shed new light upon what women search for in their intimate sexual relationships. We can also look at dynamics that frequently occur in couples and understand more clearly some of the psychological pieces that make up that puzzle.

We know that most girls are brought up looking forward to the time when they will find a man to marry. For a woman marriage is the statement of her success as a woman, and her husband's success marks her place in the social world. The couple relationship inevitably takes on enormous significance in the lives of women. This, together with a woman's search for acceptance, nurturance, and emotional continuity, means that women come to couple relationships with great expectations.

On the one hand a woman may feel that once she is married, or involved in a long-term committed relationship, at long last she is guaranteed someone to love her and to be with her. She deeply wants to feel this kind of security. She yearns to feel special to someone, for someone to connect with intimately, for someone to see her, accept her, and care for her. She feels that if she had such a person she could finally feel good about herself. Women and men alike have a need for emotional contact. Friends, co-workers, family, neighbors all play a part in fulfilling this very human need, and to greater and lesser extents people develop close and intimate relationships that are nonsexual. But for most people, deep, intimate contact—sharing our innermost thoughts and feelings, indeed our innermost sense of self, with another person—seems possible only within a sexual couple relationship.

The fabric of intimacy is woven of three elements: boundaries, dependency, and separateness.[1] When a relationship begins it may appear to be an easy process of opening oneself up, of being eager to be close to another person. At the same time each person comes to the relationship with protections and boundaries because emotional trust has not yet been built. The caring, gentleness, understanding, excitement, warmth, and concern of each partner builds trust between the two. As the trust develops in a relationship, the distance between the two people begins to disappear and the intimacy reaches a new depth. Achieving a truly satisfactory and "healthy" relationship, however, is no easy feat, for people bring with them all the complexities of their psychologies: self-protection, feelings of fear, insecurity, anger, difficulties in receiving and giving love, as well as issues of sexuality. Both partners also bring a range of expectations, even if unconscious, about who this person is going to be for them.

In our experience with couple counseling, the couple usually seeks a therapist when there is a severe crisis within the relationship that they cannot work through together. They have been suffering together for quite some time, unable to get out of the knots and tangles they feel themselves to be in. Communication has broken down considerably and each person feels misunderstood by the other. It may seem that the feelings between them which were once loving and sweet have gone sour; both are now upset, with anger and bad feelings between them. They can no longer rely on the good feelings between them.

Anne and Bob came to couple counseling because they felt that communication had become extremely poor between them. They had been together for eight years and the past three years had been difficult for them. Their sexual relationship had become almost nonexistent, they bickered regularly, and they had gotten into a pattern of continually criticizing and finding fault with one another.

In the sessions we observed that whenever moments of closeness occurred, Anne and Bob were almost instantaneously off again into another argument, with blame and fault-finding thrown back and forth between them. They came to see that actually they were quite frightened and uncomfortable in moments of closeness.

Gradually it emerged that Anne felt frightened of closeness because she feared being hurt. She recounted several incidents in which she felt Bob had hurt, rejected, or abandoned her when she was feeling vulnerable and open toward him. Bob felt frightened of closeness because he felt that he always did something that upset Anne. He was very much in the dark about why this happened and felt he was walking on eggshells trying to keep it from happening. He felt rejected, undermined, and less and less confident of his ability to give. As a result he would become angry with Anne, and this further contributed to the tension and distance between them. With each turn of this painful cycle Bob's and Anne's contact and communication diminished.

In our counseling we learned that Anne's mother and fa-

ther had a very unhappy marriage. All through Anne's childhood they fought with each other, often quite viciously.
Anne's mother would "confide" in Anne how awful her father was, how selfish and incapable of caring for anyone but
himself. The mother was so unhappy she had little to give to
Anne emotionally, and in treating her as a confidante she
denied Anne's needs as a little girl. Instead Anne came to
feel that she had to take care of her mother and try to make
her happy, to make up for all her suffering.

When Anne married Bob she was unaware of the ways
her parents' marriage had affected her. In the first years of
the marriage she felt overjoyed in her love for Bob. She felt
that he was gentle and caring and that she had found not
only a husband but a friend. She finally had someone to lean
on.

During their fourth year of marriage Bob's business went
through a difficult patch and he was very much caught up in
it. He spent longer hours at work and when he was at home
he was usually preoccupied with thoughts about work. He
became emotionally unavailable to Anne.

Bob's change of behavior resonated for Anne at an unconscious level. His inability to give emotionally and connect
with her touched the feelings of rejection and abandonment
that Anne had felt in her relationship with her mother. Just
as Anne's mother, emotionally caught up in her own marital
distress, had been unable to care for Anne adequately, now
Bob was unable to care adequately. Anne's little-girl self,
which had been vulnerable to Bob in the early years of their
marriage, went underground. Her deep unconscious fears
that she would be abandoned again seemed to be coming
true. Anne's defenses strengthened against the continued
disappointment and hurt that she now anticipated from her
husband. At the times when they still achieved some degree

of intimacy Anne's unconscious fears and expectations emerged and she looked for the ways in which Bob could disappoint and hurt her. Then, when disappointments came, Anne grasped at them and held them up to Bob as proof of her feelings that he was inadequate and couldn't take care of her.

We can use Bob and Anne's situation to illustrate a feminist approach in couple counseling. First, we see that Anne was searching for a mother in her marriage. This is something that both women and men do in all kinds of ways. Anne, needing a different experience from the one she had with her mother, looked to Bob to provide the care and nurturance her mother had not given. Anne's little-girl self first sought and found contact in her marriage and then, disappointed and rejected, went underground again, leaving distance and emotional emptiness between the couple.

Second, we understand that the messages Anne's mother gave her by her own behavior were "Do not expect emotional care from anyone," "Men are disappointments," "Men are emotionally unavailable and hurt you," "You must take care of yourself." Anne absorbed the messages and at some level anticipated rejection and abandonment from Bob. It was impossible for her to sustain the good and secure feelings about him throughout his business crisis because this abandonment was what she had unconsciously been waiting for. We can also see another dimension of women's psychology in Anne's feeling that she was in her mother's shoes—in an unhappy marriage with an emotionally unavailable man. For Anne to have a happy marriage, and a life quite different from her mother's, touched issues of psychological separation that Anne was psychologically unprepared for.

A feminist approach helped Bob to understand why his

feelings of inadequacy emerged so readily in relation to Anne and why those feelings were accompanied by strong feelings of anger. Bob's own transference issues related to his mother were clearly a part of the dynamics of the relationship. There was a psychological fit that clasped the problems between them.

Anne's difficulty in believing that she really could depend on Bob for emotional nurturance is a common problem in couple relationships. Dependency is a central issue in all relationships and is especially critical in intimate sexual relationships. At the same time that intimacy grows in a relationship, the partners are developing emotional dependency on one another. There is a recognition of caring, of emotional nurturance that is both needed and wanted. Commitment and a sense of being responsible toward the other person are facets of this dependency.

What we tend to find is that one person within the relationship, usually the woman, carries the insecurity and feelings of dependency for both partners. If one person feels insecure and very dependent, then the other person within the couple can feel quite secure, confident of not being abandoned. If one person holds tightly, the other can feel secure.

Although both men and women have difficulties with their dependency needs, it may be that the woman appears to be the dependent partner—to need the man more than he needs her—because of the dynamics of sexual politics. Men go from their mothers to another woman; by and large they have the security of a woman in their lives. They can depend on the relationship. This sense of having someone there and the security it produces allows the man in a relationship to feel more separate, to carry on activities outside the relationship confident that the woman is there waiting for him.

For the woman, however, both previous experience and

her psychology produce anxiety that she will lose the person she loves, that she will have to curb her dependency needs and not expect to be looked after emotionally: she will be pushed away. This has happened with mother. Father also comes and goes. A woman cannot have a man's expectation that the needed and loved person will be there securely for her. Because her emotional dependency needs are cut short and because she cannot then express them directly she may exhibit clinginess in an intimate relationship.[2] Because she feels insecure she may overinvolve herself in her lover's life in order to feel a secure continuity. She creates the continuity herself.

When we explore these themes in a couple-counseling situation what we usually find is that the man is just as dependent upon the woman as she is on him. Men's dependency needs are generally less recognized, because the sex-role stereotypes go very deep in our culture and shape the way we view this dynamic in couples. In our work, however, especially when the woman exhibits some autonomy and separateness, the man's insecurity and fear of losing his partner become apparent. His emotional dependency is unveiled.

People have an ability to seek each other out, to find someone with whom they "fit" psychologically. This is part of the attraction and has both positive and problematic aspects. In counseling a couple we often see that one person keeps tight boundaries while the other seems to be searching and reaching out for contact with the other. In courtship this may be part of the challenge, but in the ongoing life of the couple it can cause frustration. It is as if the boundaries have to be kept by someone. This unfortunate fit, caused by the fear of intimacy, leads to a bad spiral in which the more one person keeps up the boundaries, the more the other feels forced to push through them. However, the more the person pushes in an attempt to make contact and be close, the more the other puts up a firm wall as a defense. This dynamic confirms the fears of both people. The person who is keeping up the boundaries fears being taken over and controlled by the partner, and the partner's attempts to push through the boundaries seem to confirm this fear, since they are experienced as forceful intrusions or demands. The person who tries to make the contact fears that the partner will reject him or her and this fear is also confirmed, as are his or her feelings about being too "hungry" and demanding.

When a woman is the partner actively seeking contact, her fear of having an unending well of need inside her, of being insatiable, also seems confirmed, because the more she is kept at a distance and not given to, the more her need is felt and the greater it seems. She feels that the little-girl part of herself is unmanageable and unlovable. In turn, unprepared to provide emotional nurturance, men often feel frightened of women's needs. They feel that what is required of them is awesome and that the woman's need for emotional intimacy is indeed insatiable. A man may fear that he will be taken over or swallowed up by his partner's neediness (the unconscious resonance of his early merger with mother). The result, then, is that the man keeps firm boundaries and the woman feels shut out and hungry for contact.

For many couples this dynamic remains consistent, with each partner staying in his or her respective position. However, in certain couples this dynamic may shift back and forth as in the cha-cha,[3] in which one partner goes forward, the other goes back, and then the reverse. The shift occurs when the partner who was carrying the dependency, holding on, trying to push through the boundaries, stops and steps back. The person may step back as a result of frustration, anger, disappointment, or hopelessness about being able to reach the other partner.

As one partner retreats there is a new space between the two, a space that used to be filled with the yearnings of the partner who has retreated. In this new space several things may occur. First, the partner behind the wall experiences the absence of what was felt as pressure. More important, what is felt now is the absence of the other's attention. The solidness of the wall may dissolve slightly as the person begins to experience his or her own need for the other. He or she may now feel abandoned, frightened of losing the other, and more aware of dependent feelings, and may advance in turn or retreat further. The partner may or may not advance again in response. As we see, the whole cha-cha can be very upsetting and frustrating for both partners, because the degree of closeness each of them seeks is so hard to achieve.

These difficulties related to dependency between couples have their roots in the prescribed sex roles of our society, which do not expect boys to grow into emotionally nurturant people while girls' very sense of self is often dependent upon possessing this quality. The imbalance causes psychological damage for both sexes.

A useful way to describe the healthy model of an adult couple would be to say that each person comes to the relationship with a secure, defined, and generally positive sense of self, together with the ability to receive and give love. Because of this secure sense of self each person also brings into the relationship the ability to let the other be separate. One is not looking to the other to fill an emptiness inside. Rather, two "whole" people come together, share love and intimacy, and merge emotionally, physically, and sexually without fear. What this means is, ideally again, that each person has the ability to open up, merge, and separate without fear of loss of self or loss of the other person.

This model of the "healthy" couple is one that is not very

familiar to any of us; few couples have achieved this state. What we find in couples who are having difficulties and therefore seeking counseling is a diffused sense of boundaries, a lack of secure sense of self; each is seeking in the other the longed-for loving person he or she wants, or the longed-for self that she or he cannot be.

Since women are encouraged to find and define themselves through their relationships, a woman may look to her partner to fill parts of herself that she feels are missing. This phenomenon is often misinterpreted by Freudian therapists, who call it penis envy (see chapter 1, note 9). In reality the woman is searching for a missing part of herself.

This in itself is not unique to women. People see qualities in their loved ones that they admire and desire for themselves, which is why many couples appear from the outside to have quite opposite personality characteristics. Again this is part of the attraction, challenge, and excitement of a relationship. Each person wishes to expand and express through the relationship hidden aspects of his or her personality. However, this dynamic of projection can also cause problems because of the blurring of boundaries that sexual intimacy may produce. Each person may see an unwanted aspect of self in the other and be judgmental toward the partner. A person uneasy with his or her own vulnerability may defend against seeing it in a partner.

For example, Karen described feeling uncomfortable in social situations with Pete. She felt that Pete's comments on various things were "stupid" and she imagined that other people thought he was not very bright. She cringed every time their friends talked about current economic affairs, inflation, unemployment, and the state of the world because Pete always participated. Karen began to feel more and more anxious in these kinds of situations and began to see that there were many things she didn't really like about

Pete. She started to see him less often. When we discussed this in therapy we came to see that, in fact, Karen felt quite insecure about her own participation in those discussions and her anxieties were due to her unconscious merger with Pete. She felt that she "covered" herself adequately, that she knew how to "say enough without exposing ignorance." But she felt that Pete did not do this, and, because of her own unclear boundaries, each time he spoke up it was she who felt exposed. She had had to distance herself from the relationship to maintain her sense of control and boundaries.

As well as this dynamic of projection, there is a tendency in couples to transmit their hopes, desires, expectations, and anxieties to each other. The sensitivity that seems to go along with sexual relationships is not usually found in friendships. In friendships people are often able to contain their feelings "appropriately," but in sexual relationships the boundaries that have been crossed physically seem to open more paths and avenues that the emotions traverse. Unspoken and unrecognized demands, assumptions, and expectations are bound up in the sexual relationship, so that feelings of disappointment or anger are easily triggered, often without the lover's knowledge or awareness.

Difficulties with merger and separateness are noticeable when differences are exposed. One partner may transmit his or her views on a particular topic or experience to the other, assuming that they are mirrored by the partner, and be extraordinarily upset to discover they are not. Or one partner may have difficulty in exposing his or her differences. When one's partner is in disagreement or does not support one's own view, it can feel like a personal injury. If one has unconsciously assumed that the lover is an extension of oneself, a difference of opinion that suddenly outlines each person's boundaries is jarring.

In couple counseling the therapist is trying to help the two people uncover their hidden expectations and assumptions so that a clearer communication can take place between them. A feminist approach brings a particular awareness about matters of psychological separateness and merger.

In addition, within heterosexual relationships both the man and the woman have assumptions and expectations that arise from sex-role stereotyping in patriarchal society. Some of these are obvious but that does not mean that they are not deeply embedded in our psychologies. For example, a woman's desire for a "strong" man or a man's desire for a "gentle, caring" woman will find expression in the relationship. The feminist therapist will bear these cultural stereotypes in mind and use them as an important part of the work of helping a couple achieve a more equal, interdependent intimacy.

Lesbian relationships also raise the same issues of intimacy, boundaries, dependency, and separateness, but in a different way. First and most important, in a lesbian relationship there is a tension about being in a relationship that is not accepted within the culture at large. Although many of the emotional dynamics are similar to those of heterosexual partners, the context of the relationship is bound to be different. Laws of patriarchal culture allow for heterosexual love and outlaw sexual love between women. For a lesbian couple there is the constant threat of the culture coming into the context of the relationship and bringing with it condemnation, punishment, attacks of shame and guilt. There is, even in the 1980s, little support for lesbian couples apart from within the lesbian community. It is therefore very difficult for lesbians to expose the problems within their relationship because the general response is still to see these problems as having to do with the sexual choice rather than the emotional dynamics between the women in the couple.

186

This, of course, is not generally offered as a reason for heterosexual couples' problems; no one is likely to suggest that having chosen to be heterosexual might be what is causing the trouble.

Matters of boundaries and closeness have a different tone when there are two women involved. In our experience many mother-daughter dynamics cross from one partner to the other within lesbian relationships. Issues that arise include those of a woman attempting to define herself as separate from another woman; trying to experience herself as different from her lover; expressing, giving, and receiving love from another woman; and the inevitable projections and identifications that occur between two women who are close. Perhaps the fear of merger with another woman heightens the unconscious memory of the earlier relationship with mother.

In lesbian relationships there are two "little-girls" as well as two potential "mothers" in the situation. Each woman brings to the relationship her little-girl self, yearning to be loved, cared for, accepted, and validated by another woman. But, as we have seen, the little-girl inside also brings feelings of tremendous neediness; anxieties about rejection, abandonment, and disappointment; and feelings of anger. Lesbian relationships contain the possibility of nurture and love shared between two women. Since both women have been raised to "mother"—to care for others—there may be a reciprocal nurturance.

In couple counseling we see the difficulties lesbian women have in coping with each other's little-girl selves. Because most women have trouble accepting that part of themselves, they defend against the exposure of the little-girl inside. This is no less true in lesbian relationships, where often both women are trying to curb their own neediness at the same

187

time that the needs of the lover are stimulating their own. There may be an identification between the two little-girls inside that is difficult for the partners to accept and deal with. A feminist therapist tries to help the two women express and accept their own emotional needs as well as those of their lovers, so that the appropriate caring can take place.

Other dynamics that we see in lesbian relationships are those of women's relationships in general: envy, competition, feelings of betrayal and anger. In a lesbian couple there are two women with women's psychology, and many of the aspects we discussed in chapter 7 are present in the relationship. The sexual relationship often adds to the intensity of these feelings.

Above all, feminist therapists must be aware of the social and political difficulties facing lesbian couples. Only with that awareness on the part of the therapist can a lesbian couple seek counseling without the threat that their choice of partner will be placed in the forefront of their problems.

Both lesbian and heterosexual relationships embody issues of autonomy and intimacy. The issue of women's separateness presents itself more obviously as a problem in contemporary relationships since the women's movement brought about changes in consciousness. Because women and men experience both consciously and unconsciously women's separateness as something to be feared (see chapter 2), couples may unconsciously collude to keep the woman restrained. Her autonomy produces difficulty. Both men's and women's first dependent and primary relationship was with a woman, and we all carry a sore spot of fear of abandonment and loss of a woman. A woman's autonomy in a couple arouses these deeply held feelings. This is just as resonant and true for lesbian couples.

In couple counseling, once a woman's neediness is no longer seen to be the major problem (which it is so often thought to be at first), we then see many of the feelings that men have about their own inadequacy in nurturing and in relating intimately. We may find that the man gets very frightened when he sees that the woman is upset or angry with him; he may try to protect himself and defend against his own vulnerability. He may feel like a little boy being told he has disappointed or upset his mother. He may not know how to give or what to give. Often men's vulnerability and feelings of inadequacy are converted into anger. The anger operates as a defense to cover up the vulnerable feelings and protect them from exposure. This anger illustrates another common psychological fit in heterosexual couples. The man's defensive anger entwines with the woman's fear of anger and her feelings of unentitlement. The anger may discourage her from pursuing what she feels she wants.

Our overall goal in counseling is for both people within the relationship to recognize their love and need for one another, and at the same time be able to enjoy psychological separateness and autonomy. Achieving such healthy intimate relationships—relationships in which both people are equal and interdependent—has fundamental implications for the structure of the family unit. Heterosexual relationships, the core of the family, are still generally built on inequalities between men and women. In chapter 10 we shall move on to speculate about the future if dramatic changes toward equality were to occur in the psychology of women and men.

Notes

1. See Luise Eichenbaum and Susie Orbach, *What Do Women Want? Exploding the Myth of Dependency,* New York, 1983.
   In our postgraduate training workshops at The Women's Therapy Centre,

we have used this outline in helping psychotherapists sensitize themselves to couple dynamics:

I. *Intimacy.* Why is intimacy so difficult to achieve? What are the fears associated with emotional intimacy?

a. Psychological fits: What attracts people to one another? Are there emotional fits that work/do not work between people?

b. Boundary issues: Does one person keep tight boundaries as a protection against intimacy while the other partner reaches out in search of contact? Does intimacy feel like merger and loss of self? Does one person "take over" and possess the other? Is it possible for a couple to consist of two whole, separated people?

c. The cha-cha phenomenon.

II. *Dependency.* Why does it so often seem that one person is more dependent in the relationship than the other partner? In heterosexual relationships why is this person more often than not the woman? Is it possible to achieve interdependency in intimate relationships? What issues does the therapist take up, and how?

a. The effect of women's lack of separateness in couples: Does the woman's lack of separateness provide the safety net for the man to be more separate?

b. Do men's difficulties with nurturing hamper women's activities away from home and in the world?

c. Do women's autonomy and psychological separateness affect relationships? What is their impact?

III. *Sexuality.* What are the difficulties in achieving sexual intimacy? Are the issues the same in lesbian and heterosexual intimacy? If not, what are the differences? Where does sex fit into intimacy? How do women's and men's deep feelings about female sexuality affect their sexual relationships?

IV. *Countertransference.* What is aroused in the therapist about the woman's expression of her needs? Does the therapist (male or female) identify with either partner in the couple? We have supervised many therapists who unwittingly reinforce the disequilibrium between the sexes. Both men and women therapists may not anticipate that a man will be emotionally articulate or vulnerable and, when he does speak openly about his feelings, that may be a kind of end point for the therapist who feels pleased that the male client has shown a "part of himself." The therapist may feel that the work was successful because it extracted something from the man and that the woman client should feel satisfied. Like the woman client, the therapist may feel that a woman should not expect too much emotionally from a man (see chapter 2) and that her continued wanting means that her needs are overwhelming. She or he may feel that the role of the couple counselor is to help the man articulate a little more and to help the woman accept his limitations and curb her neediness.

2. Most interpretations in traditional psychoanalysis and couple counseling view the dynamics in a woman's relationship with a male partner as transference having to do with her father. This reductionist view often misses the central point.

3. See Eichenbaum and Orbach, *What Do Women Want?*

CHAPTER 10

Looking Forward

THE kind of theory we have been presenting sees psychic structure as fluid rather than immutable. It is constructed under particular conditions in a particular way. The present psychic structure of women derives from current child-rearing arrangements in which women bring up the children of a patriarchal society, and it is based on a translation of culture, material conditions, actual personal relationships, power relationships within the family, and the psychodynamics of relationships.

We believe that psychic structural changes at a fundamental and a mass level will arise only from a change in the material conditions in which children are raised, and from a change in the social position of women. In this chapter we discuss both the changing position of women and ways of changing individual psychology, because these two issues play an important part in breaking the cycle of damaging self-hatred that operates from generation to generation of women.

The process of uncovering the ways in which femininity is reproduced has gone hand in hand with the activities and the vision of the women's movement. The women's movement has opened the way to seeing how the tragic cycle of socialization from mothers to daughters can begin to be broken. New forms of child rearing and family relationships are emerging as we begin to understand that the way "women are made"[1] is inextricably bound up with women's social position. As Adrienne Rich writes, in *Of Woman Born*: "A woman who has respect and affection for her own body, who does not view it as unclean or as a sex object, will wordlessly transmit to her daughter that a woman's body is a good and healthy place to live. A woman who feels pride in being female will not visit her self-depreciation upon her female children."[2]

Women's social position, and hence their experience of self, will take several generations to change. In the meantime we argue for the equal involvement of both parents in the raising of children and for the presence of both sexes in the early life of children. We need male caregivers and nursery-school teachers, for example. If there is no move toward balance between the sexes, the general position of women—even if individually some women may escape the dreadful feelings of unworthiness and self-doubt—and the reproduction of the feminine psychic structure we have described will not change.

The kind of structural psychological shifts that we think necessary cannot be sufficiently implemented in one generation. Women and men currently carry with them deep feelings of misogyny and unconscious sexism. Even with changes in child-rearing arrangements, these influences will have their impact on at least the first generation raised by two parents, for, as we have seen, psychological development involves the embodying of the psychologies of our first caregivers. This is said not to be discouraging but rather to stress the seriousness of the project at hand, and to emphasize the necessity of the long-term approach to such structural changes.

Changes in the family and in child-rearing practices will affect women's psychology and development in many ways.

With fathers involved in the raising of children, the psychology of the father himself will alter. Men too will have to change radically and develop areas of themselves that are as yet unexplored. They will have to experience the feelings of inadequacy, anxiety, and vulnerability that accompany the necessary opening up to, taking in, and learning about the skills of nurturance. They will expose their vulnerability as they develop and express that part of themselves. Men learning to become nurturers and fathers will, of course, dramatically affect the psyches of the children who are being raised. Being raised by a father as well as a mother will be vastly different from traditional mothering. The male child will be able to develop a sense of gender by identifying with his father. In our present society a boy develops his sense of self in opposition to his mother, who is female and "other."[3] In the future we envision boys will develop a secure sense of themselves as male that does not depend on establishing defensive differences with women. The psychology that the boy embodies will contain the psychologies of both his parents. His positive experiences will relate to both sexes, as will his negative ones. He will experience the power of nurturance, boundary drawing, and restrictions from a man as well as a woman. He will have strong feelings of love as well as anger and hate toward both a man and a woman. These changes will contribute to the transformation of the misogynist nature of masculine psychology.

Boys being raised by a father as well as a mother will be allowed and encouraged to develop their own nurturing abilities in previously unknown ways. Seeing his father, a male engaged in nurturing and domestic activities, the boy will come to feel that this too is his world, and he will bring a nurturing self both to his relationships with his family and peers and to his intimate sexual relationships.

UNDERSTANDING WOMEN

A little girl raised by both a father and a mother will also have a radically different psychology. First of all, she will have an early close relationship with father. Fathers, and hence men, will lose their mystique—they will no longer be seen as remote and unknowable. Emotionality will become associated with both sexes, and the girl will grow into a woman who has a reasonable expectation of receiving emotional nurturance and emotional consistency from men.

Two parenting adults can create dramatic changes in feminine psychic structural development during the period of infantile dependency. We have seen that the nurturance girls receive in this period is at present extremely staccato and contains a push-pull dynamic leading to a fundamental feeling of insecurity and lack of self-esteem. If the period of infantile dependency is no longer the responsibility of one parent who is both over- and undervalued in her role as mother and is herself a needy person, but is instead an experience shared by two confident, mature adults, then what the infant embodies from them in the process of becoming a person will be very different.

The joyful nature of parenting shared in this way will be communicated and transmitted to the baby. Nurturance, confidence, pleasure, and wholesome engagement will be a part of the relating. The baby's contentment and security will be communicated back to the parents, contributing to their confidence and pleasure in the parenting process.

In at least the first generation of children raised by both parents, however, the mother's psychology and the father's psychology that the girl child embodies will reflect aspects of a mother's negative self-image and neediness and a father's fear and misogyny. Mother may feel less needy because she does not have sole responsibility for her child and she can feel the support of her partner, but this will not dispel all her feelings of deprivation and confusions about her entitle-

194

ments. Similarly, the first generation of fathers who nurture will feel somewhat hesitant and nervous in their new role. They may transmit feelings of inadequacy and resentment to their children.

But let us move on several generations and project the new psychic structure for girls. If two parents are rearing children together we can assume that it will be easier for them to cope with a child's distress. At present a baby girl's distress brings up a mother's special identification with her own distress and reflects her fears of bad mothering; her attempts to alleviate her daughter's pain are tinged with the desire to push it away. Two parents, neither of whom over-identifies with the daughter, may enable the infant girl to tolerate painful experiences and so come to feel she can survive them, and also to feel that her feelings are not dangerous.

At a psychic structural level, the child's negative experiences will not all be centered around mother. Just as the girl (and the boy) embodies two parents in the positive nurturing experiences that promote ego development, so too will the negative and difficult experiences be associated with two parents, two people with different genders. All badness will no longer derive from experiences of disappointment with women. The implications for the eradication of feminine misogyny are profound, because the girl will not have the deeply embedded sense that at bottom what mother is, what she herself is and can be, what all women are, is at once all good and all bad.[4]

The change from distrust of women to trust will be paralleled with a change in how girls see women and men in their sex roles. Because both men and women would be involved in the domestic labor that is so much a part of daily life, little girls and boys learning domestic skills would not see them as second-class work; they would be seen, rightly we believe, as a necessary part of life, rather than falsely under- or over-valued. The sense of sexual inequality that attaches to the division of labor would change, creating a shift in a woman's self-esteem. She would come to feel that she is a participant in human activity rather than someone whose work is both invisible and misvalued.

The change from women's sole responsibility for the household and child rearing would have to be accompanied by a change in employment possibilities for women and men and a restructuring of the labor process. This in turn would have an impact on a girl's experience of womanhood. A child growing up in an environment where both parents have commitments at work and outside the family will have a very different sense of who both women and men are and what to expect of them.

The kinds of changes we are advocating will not occur without tremendous upheaval at both a psychological and a social level. For example, it is unrealistic to think that a woman could easily relinquish the power and impact she currently has in the family: the organization of the household and the control and socialization of the children. Even when an important outside interest engaged her, she might well feel a loss of self-definition and social standing as she moved outside her self-image of femininity. As a woman gives up some of her control she may experience a sense of loss and disorientation; she may feel embarrassed and humiliated at her partner's taking on aspects of a social role previously deemed correct for her, incorrect for him. Similarly, men who have the best intentions and a commitment to a restructuring of sexual politics may feel inadequate, clumsy, and out of place in their new role as nurturers and equal partners.

The possibility of girls and boys being raised by both parents will have a profound impact on the psychological profiles of femininity and masculinity. Girls and boys will have the chance to develop the nurturing aspect of themselves—not from a position of neediness, as is now so often the case with girls, or defensiveness, which is how men under pressure develop nurturing qualities, but from a position of having received an unambiguous, wholesome, well-nurtured childhood.

Girls today rarely achieve psychological separation, and boys' psychological separation is imbued with a deep defensiveness. In subsequent generations both girls and boys will achieve psychological separation from their parents through strength and a sense of wholeness. The melting of false boundaries in both sexes will occur with an authentic experience of selfhood. Girls' and boys' psychic structures will reflect the embodiment of positive and negative experiences with both women and men. Mother will no longer represent the person who has the power to give all or withhold all. Intimacy will include rich experiences with father, and mother's image will necessarily be modified.

The new ways of relating that these changes will bring about are as yet unforeseeable. We can guess at the outlines but only barely glimpse the details of the wealth of possibilities in friendship, sexual relations, and parenting. In friendship perhaps all women will be able to achieve what has begun to be achieved as a result of the women's movement: honest, loving relationships, built not on fear, betrayal, competition, or envy, and not on solidarity in opposition to men, but on sharing, contact between equals, and support for autonomy. In friendships between women and men we can look forward to an equal exchange of emotionality and strength. Friendships between men will allow for a disclosure of self and the knowledge that men can nurture and support each other.

In heterosexual relations we can foresee a coming together

of a woman and a man on the basis of two separate and autonomous people seeking intimacy. Neither of them fears women, and the woman is free of the mystery that surrounds "having a man." With psychological separateness and economic independence, women and men can relate to one another on the basis of equal exchange, rather than that of the man providing financial security and the woman emotional nurturance. It will be possible for both partners to recognize their dependency on each other, to share their emotional world and abandon the cha-cha dynamic (see chapter 9). The respect a woman will feel for herself means that she will not need to seek confirmation of her self-worth through a man's approval. Similarly, a man's secure knowledge of his own boundaries will not force him to present himself in opposition to a woman.

In lesbian relationships we can look forward to two strong, loved women giving to each other, not from neediness or overidentification and with resentment, but on the basis of appreciation in loving a woman who is like oneself but also separate. In male homosexual relationships we can speculate that certain painful aspects of self-hatred and animosity toward women will dissolve, so that the love men feel for each other can flourish.

The kinds of changes we are projecting are a glimpse down one particular pathway. The recontextualizing of our lives, the struggle against patriarchy, will require social upheaval spread over many generations. In our time there has been a profound questioning of the nuclear family, which has been accompanied by an acceleration in divorce, single parenting, communal living, and cooperative communities. Some of these divergences and new ways of parenting have been pursued intentionally,[5] while some are still practiced with the image of and desire for the nuclear family in mind.

It will be several generations before the effects of the new parenting arrangements on psychic structure can be assessed, and this will require a sensitive understanding of the many diverse paths that people are now exploring.

Notes

1. Simone de Beauvoir, *The Second Sex*, New York, 1952.
2. Adrienne Rich, *Of Woman Born*, New York, 1976, p. 245.
3. See Robert J. Stoller, *Sex and Gender*, New York, 1968, London, 1969.
4. Dorothy Dinnerstein, *The Mermaid and the Minotaur; Sexual Arrangements and Human Malaise*, New York, 1976.
5. See Diane Ehrensaft, "When Women and Men Mother," *Socialist Review*, January 1980, pp. 837–73.

BIBLIOGRAPHY

Arcana, Judith, *Our Mother Daughters,* Berkeley, Calif., 1979.
Aries, Philippe, *Centuries of Childhood: A Social History of Family Life,* New York, 1960.

Badinter, Elizabeth, *Mother Love,* New York, 1981.
Baker Miller, Jean, *Psychoanalysis and Women,* London, 1973.
Baker Miller, Jean, *Towards a New Psychology of Women,* Boston, Mass., 1976.
Balint, Alice, *The Early Years of Life: A Psychoanalytic Study,* New York, 1954.
Balint, M., *Primary Love and Psycho-analytic Technique,* London, 1965.
Barber, Virginia and Skaggs, Merrill Maguire, *The Mother Person,* New York, 1977.
Bardwick, Judith, *Psychology of Women: A Study of Bio-cultural Conflicts,* New York, 1971.
Belotti, Elena Giannini, *Little Girls,* New York, 1977.
Bernard, Jessie, *The Future of Marriage,* New York, 1972.
Bernard, Jessie, *The Future of Motherhood,* New York, 1974.
Blanck and Blanck, *Ego Psychology: Theory and Practice,* New York, 1974.
Bowlby, John, *Attachment and Loss,* Vols. 1 and 2, New York, 1969, 1973.
Broverman, I. K., Vogel, S. R., Broverman, D. M., Clarkson, F. E. and Rosenkrantz, P. S., 'Sex Role Stereotypes: A Current Appraisal', *Journal of Social Issues,* Vol. 28, No. 2, 1972, pp. 59–78.
Brown, Bruce, *Marx, Freud and the Critique of Everyday Life,* New York, 1973.
Brownmiller, Susan, *Against Our Will. Men, Women and Rape,* Los Angeles, Calif., 1975.

Chasseguet-Smirgel, Janine, *Female Sexuality,* Ann Arbor, Mich., 1970.
Chesler, Phyllis, *Women and Madness,* New York, 1972.
Chodorow, Nancy, *The Reproduction of Mothering: Psychoanalysis and the Sociology of Gender,* Berkeley, Calif., 1978.

Daly, A., *Mothers,* London, 1976.
de Beauvoir, Simone, *The Second Sex,* New York, 1952.
Deutsch, Helene, *The Psychology of Women,* Vols. 1 and 2, New York, 1944, 1945.
Dinnerstein, Dorothy, *The Mermaid and the Minotaur; Sexual Arrangements and Human Malaise,* New York, 1976.

200

Bibliography

Engels, Friedrich, *The Origin of the Family, Private Property and the State,* New York, 1973.

Erikson, Erik, 'Womanhood and the Inner Space' in Robert Jay Lifton (ed.), *The Woman in America,* Boston, Mass., 1964.

Ernst, Sheila, and Goodison, Lucy, *In Our Own Hands,* London, 1981.

Fairbairn, W. R. D., *Psychoanalytic Studies of the Personality,* London, 1952.

Fenichel, O., *Psychoanalytic Theory of Neurosis,* New York, 1945.

Foucault, Michel, *The History of Sexuality,* Vol. I. *An Introduction,* New York, 1978.

Freud, Anna, *The Ego and the Mechanisms of Defense,* New York, 1966.

Freud, Sigmund, *The Complete Psychological Works,* New York, 1964.

Freud, Sigmund, *Three Essays on the Theory of Sexuality,* New York, 1963.

Friday, Nancy, *My Mother, My Self,* New York, 1977.

Friedan, Betty, *The Feminine Mystique,* New York, 1963.

Frieze, Parsons, Johnson, Ruble, Zellman, *Women and Sex Roles. A Social Psychological Perspective,* New York, 1978.

Gagnon, John H., and Simon, William, *Sexual Conduct: The Social Sources of Human Sexuality,* Chicago, 1973.

Garfield Barback, Lonnie, *For Yourself: The Fulfillment of Female Sexuality,* New York, 1975.

Gilligan, Carol, *In a Different Voice,* Cambridge, Mass., 1982.

Gornick, Vivian, and Moran, Barbara K. (eds.), *Woman in Sexist Society: Studies in Power and Powerlessness,* New York, 1971.

Guntrip, Harry, *Personality Structure and Human Interaction: The Developing Synthesis of Psychodynamic Theory,* New York, 1964.

Guntrip, Harry, *Schizoid Phenomena and Object Relations Theory,* New York, 1969.

Guntrip, Harry, *Psychoanalytic Theory, Therapy and the Self,* New York, 1971.

Hammer, Signe, *Daughters and Mothers, Mothers and Daughters,* New York, 1975.

Hammer, Signe, *Women, Body and Culture,* New York, 1975.

Hartmann, Heinz, *Ego Psychology and the Problem of Adaptation,* New York, 1958.

Hershberger, Ruth, *Adam's Rib,* New York, 1948.

Hite, Shere, *The Hite Report,* New York, 1976.

Horney, Karen, *Feminine Psychology,* New York, 1967.

Howell, Elizabeth, and Bayes, Marjorie, eds., *Women and Mental Health,* New York, 1981.

Jacobson, Edith, *The Self and the Object World,* New York, 1964.

Jacoby, Russell, *Social Amnesia,* Boston, Mass., 1976.

Bibliography

Kaplan, J. L., *Oneness and Separateness, From Infant to Individual,* New York, 1978.

Kernberg, Otto, *Borderline Conditions and Pathological Narcissism,* New York, 1975.

Kernberg, Otto, *Object Relations Theory and Clinical Psychoanalysis,* New York, 1976.

Klein, George S., *Freud's Two Theories of Sexuality: Psychological Issues,* No. 9.

Klein, Melanie, *The Psycho-analysis of Children,* New York, 1932.

Klein, Melanie, *Envy and Gratitude,* New York, 1975.

Klein, Melanie, *Love, Guilt and Reparation,* New York, 1975.

Klein, Melanie, et al., *Developments in Psychoanalysis,* London, 1952.

Lazarre, Jane, *The Mother Knot,* New York, 1976.

Lerner, Harriet, "Early Origins of Envy and Devaluation of Women: Implications for Sex-Role Stereotypes," *Bulletin of the Menninger Clinic,* Vol. 38, No. 6, 1974.

Lerner, Harriet, "Internal Prohibitions Against Female Anger," *The American Journal of Psychoanalysis,* Vol. 40, No. 2, 1980.

Maccoby, Eleanor, and Jacklin, Carol, *The Psychology of Sex Differences,* Stanford, Calif., 1974.

Mahler, Margaret, *On Human Symbiosis and the Vicissitudes of Individuation,* New York, 1964.

Mahler, Margaret S., Pine, Fred, and Bergman, Anni, *The Psychological Birth of the Human Infant: Symbiosis and Individuation,* New York, 1975.

Masters, William H., and Johnson, Virginia E., *Human Sexual Response,* Boston, Mass., 1966.

Mead, Margaret, *Male and Female,* New York, 1968.

Miller, Alice, *Prisoners of Childhood,* New York, 1981.

Millett, Kate, *Sexual Politics,* New York, 1971.

Mitchell, Juliet, *Women's Estate,* New York, 1973.

Mitchell, Juliet, *Psychoanalysis and Feminism,* New York, 1974.

Money, John, and Erhardt, Anke, *Man and Woman, Boy and Girl: The Differentiation and Dimorphism of Gender Identity from Conception to Maturity,* Baltimore, Md., 1973.

Money, John, and Tucker, Patricia, *Sexual Signatures: On Being a Man or a Woman,* Boston, Mass., 1975.

Oakley, Ann, *Sex, Gender and Society,* New York, 1973.

Orbach, Susie, *Fat is a Feminist Issue,* New York, 1978.

Orbach, Susie, *Fat is a Feminist Issue II,* London, 1982.

Person, Ethel, *Sexuality as the mainstay of identity: Psychoanalytic perspectives, Signs,* Summer 1980, 605-630.

Reich, Wilhelm, *Character Analysis,* New York, 1972.

Bibliography

Reich, Wilhelm, *The Mass Psychology of Fascism,* New York, 1970.

Reich, Wilhelm, *The Sexual Revolution,* New York, 1974.

Reich, Wilhelm, and Teschitz, K., *Selected Sex-Pol Essays, 1934-37,* London, 1973.

Reitz, Rosetta, *Menopause: A Positive Approach,* Radnor, Penn., 1977.

Rich, Adrienne, *Of Woman Born: Motherhood as Experience and Institution,* New York, 1976.

Schneider, Michael, *Neurosis and Civilization: A Marxist-Freudian Synthesis,* New York, 1975.

Searles, Harold F., *Collected Papers on Schizophrenia and Related Subjects,* New York, 1966.

Segal, Hanna, *Introduction to the Work of Melanie Klein,* London, 1964.

Sharpe, Sue, *Just Like a Girl: How Girls Learn to be Women,* London, 1976.

Sherfey, Mary Jane, *The Nature and Evolution of Female Sexuality,* New York, 1966.

Shuttle, Penelope, and Redgrove, Peter, *Wise Wound: Eve's Curse and EveryWoman,* 1978.

Spitz, Rene A., *The First Year of Life: A Psychoanalytic Study of Normal and Deviant Development of Object Relations,* New York, 1965.

Stoller, Robert J., *Sex and Gender: On the Development of Masculinity and Femininity,* New York, 1968.

Stoller, Robert J., *Splitting: A Case of Female Masculinity,* New York, 1973.

Strouse, Jean, *Women and Analysis,* New York, 1974.

Sullivan, Harry Stack, *The Interpersonal Theory of Psychiatry,* New York, 1953.

Thompson, Clara, *Psychoanalysis: Evolution and Development,* New York, 1957.

Thompson, Clara, *On Women,* New York, 1964.

Thompson, Clara, *Interpersonal Psychoanalysis: The Selected Papers of Clara Thompson,* New York, 1964.

Weideger, Paula, *Female Cycles,* New York, 1975.

Williams, Elizabeth Friar, *Notes of a Feminist Therapist,* New York, 1977.

Winnicott, D. W., *The Child, the Family and the Outside World,* London, 1964.

Winnicott, D. W., *The Maturational Processes and the Facilitating Environment,* New York, 1965.

Winnicott, D. W., *The Family and Individual Development,* New York, 1965.

Winnicott, D. W., *Primary Maternal Preoccupation: Collected Papers,* London, 1978.

Zaretsky, Eli, *Capitalism, the Family and Personal Life,* New York, 1976.

Zimbalist Rosaldo, Michelle, and Lamphere, Louise, *Woman, Culture and Society,* Stanford, Calif., 1974.

INDEX

adolescence: father-daughter relationship in, 65–66; female sexuality and, 58–59; peer groups in, 117

agoraphobia, 164–65, 174n1

anger: as a defense mechanism, 189; father-daughter relationships and, 64–65; guilt regarding feelings of, 149–50; projection of, 160; separation and, 150–52

anorexia nervosa, 169, 172–74

anxiety, obsessional, 167–69

autonomy: in couple counseling, 188; dependency needs and, 103; in group therapy, 119–20; guilt in exercising, 147; intimacy and, 103, 176, 183–84, 197–98; lack of support for female, 139; psychotherapist as model for, 124; terminating psychotherapy and, 104–7, *see also* separation-individuation

Balint, M., 71

Bart, Pauline, 4–5

Beauvoir, Simone de, 144

Belotti, Elena Giannini, 10, 36

Berry, Sally, *viii*

Bloom, Carol, *ix*

boundaries: in couple counseling, 184–86; intimacy and, 176, 181–83; in lesbian relationships, 187; in mother-son relationships, 41, 57

British Object Relations School, 13

Broverman, I. K., 4–5

bulimia, 169, 172

Chesler, Phyllis, 4

Index

sciousness-raising groups
and, 5, 26n7, 123, 135–36;
countertransference in,
76–77, 122–23; defense
mechanisms in, 78–84,
85n6, 94–100; dependency
needs changes in, 102–4;
disappointment in, 94–96;
emotions of therapist in,
134–36; envy in, 145; gender identity and, 84n3;
identification in, 122–27;
integration of "little-girl"
needs and, 101–3; intimacy
in, 126; middle stage of,
86–100; power differential
in, 128–30, 133; "presenting problem" in, 73, 74;
process of, 70; push-pull
in, 99–100, 108n23; self-
disclosure of therapist in,
123–25; sexuality in, 130–
32; terminating relation-
ship in, 97–98, 100–7,
108n8, 124; therapist
needs in, 126–27; therapist
role in early stages, 72–75,
84n4; transference in, 70–
72, 93–94, 122–27; trust in,
77; women caring for therapists in, 93–94, 105–6,
123–24; workshop sessions
and, 110
push-pull: dependency needs
in, 91–92; in mother-
daughter relationships, 44,
48, 55–56, 62, 90–91, 105,

194; in psychotherapeu-
tic relationship, 99–100,
108n23

receiving, women's difficulty
with, 152–54
Rich, Adrienne, 10, 60, 192

Second Sex, The (de Beau-
voir), 144
self-worth, fantasy and, 140–
41
separation-individuation, 20–
21; adult difficulty in, 19–
20, 96; agoraphobia and,
164–65; anger and, 150–52;
difficulties in, and change,
197; father-daughter relationship and, 21–22, 62,
65–66; father's role in, 21–
22; gender identity and,
54, 57; in group therapy,
119–20; guilt and, 146–47;
in infancy, 16–17, 20–21,
52–56, 91–92; intimacy
and, 103, 176, 183–84,
197–98; mother-daughter
relationship and, 47, 52–
56, 106; in psychothera-
peutic relationships, 97–
98, 100–7, 108n8, 124; sexuality and, 59–60, 155–56;
see also autonomy
"Sex-Role Stereotypes in
Clinical Judgements of
Mental Health" (Brover-
man et al.), 4–5

Index

31n13, 66n1, 71, 96, 108n5
wives: gender identities of, 5-6; motherhood and, 6; responsibilities of, 6
women's liberation movement: consciousness-raising groups in, 3-4; impact of, 4-5
Women's Therapy Centre, The, *vii, viii, ix, x,* 109, 133
workshops, theme-centered, 109-13; on competition, 144; feelings in, 112; group therapy experience in, 110-11; support in, 111-13; topics of, 109-10; transference in, 112-13